The Navigator

Develop Founder Skills to Lead Your Startup Successfully

The Navigator

Develop Founder Skills to Lead Your Startup Successfully

My-Tien Vo

Nine Spheres
2018

NINE SPHERES
The Navigator
Develop Founder Skills to Lead Your Startup Successfully
My-Tien Vo

Art Director: Laura J. Testa-Reyes, Catalyst Creations West

First Printing 2018. Updated June 2019; updated August 2020.
Printed in the United States of America

Published in the United States of America by Nine Spheres
ISBN-13: 978-0-9982976-1-3

1. Founder Development. 2. Founder Competency. 3. Founder IQ. 4. Founder's Integrated Approach. 5. Founder's Integrated Mindset. 6. Startups. 7. New Business. 8. Entrepreneurship. The Immediacy Mindset. 10. Founder Leadership.

To my parents

Contents

Preface

You may have a great business idea that compels you to think about starting your own business. Before you do, I encourage you to spend some time reflecting and answering this question, "What founder skills and qualities do I need to possess in order to begin well and increase my chance of success?"

This question is not apparent to most first-time founders, who obsess over their business idea and operate from the view that if their product can sell and scale, they can raise money and are on their way to creating a company and profiting from it.

Clearly, there's no new business if there's no viable product. That said, an exciting product idea has no chance of success if the new founder fails at the helm as its skipper.

I've spent two decades in the startup trenches as a serial founder and collaborator with founders and co-founders. I've worn different hats during my entrepreneurial career: startup strategist, brand strategist, product developer, researcher, team builder, client relations director, operations manager, and crisis manager. I can speak to entrepreneurial success and failure.

Time and again, I've witnessed first-time founders fail not because they didn't have a great product idea. Some did. There was a founder-CTO who developed a software that was the precursor to Google Street View. Another founder came up with a community-building platform called Circles, a few years before Google added Google+ to its product portfolio. A third founder developed a service that delivered private and trackable messages.

These entrepreneurs failed because they had spent most of their time in the Product room and missed the big picture: a successful startup operation comprises many components that need to synchronize and move forward as one engine. They had overlooked the need to develop their founder role to lead and build not just their product team but their entire company successfully.

I wrote *The Navigator* because I wanted to help new entrepreneurs acquire essential founder skills and avoid this most common and far-reaching oversight.

If you're thinking about starting a new company, this book is for you. Train yourself and develop your Founder IQ so you will be well prepared for your venture.

Introduction

Picture your entrepreneurial journey as a sea voyage. Your product is your offering to the world. First you need to build it. Then you need a vessel to transport your cargo and a qualified skipper at the helm. As founder, you are the captain in charge of this vessel. How well you navigate your startup will determine its future.

If you're like most first-time founders, you probably possess expertise in your profession. You begin with exuberance, high hopes, and the expectation that all you need are a good idea, startup funds, faith, smarts, hard work, and persistence.

You can "practice" as an entrepreneur without formal training, certification, or licensing. Scientists, physicians, lawyers, and accountants—on the other hand—must obtain credentials in advance and cannot practice until certified; they also learn on the job. A license ensures high and enforced standards of minimum performance; this protects the public. But no legal barriers prevent you from becoming a founder. You (or anyone) can start a business and learn by doing. That's the upside. The flip side is you can set off on your venture even if you lack skills and qualifications. Your only assurance is what you know and what you can do.

You may have a head start if you've enrolled in an entrepreneurship program, if you've grown up around entrepreneurs, or if you have start-up experience. But there's a difference between joining a startup as an employee and founding a startup. It takes an array of knowledge, experience, wisdom, and skill sets to launch and build a business—whether it's a brick-and-mortar retailer, a manufacturer of goods, a service-oriented firm, or an online store.

While many first-time founders possess knowledge and skills that enable them to start a business, most lack experience and training to run one. I was an untrained founder. I've also worked with smart professionals in hospitality, law, software, retail services, healthcare, and professional services who failed as founders because they didn't know what they didn't know.

As captain, you need to be competent before setting sail. You don't have to be an expert in how to tie rigging, but you do need to know seamanship. This means knowing how to navigate; hire and manage your crew; allocate and monitor resources; solve unanticipated problems; handle rough waters and storms; and ensure that your cargo and people reach port.

Most new entrepreneurs possess a significant blind spot. They lack an integrated view of their entire journey and have tunnel vision from the start: they operate from inside the product bubble. They're inspired by seasoned investors who are driven by a product-centric mindset: create product, find buyers, build a market for it, and then find investors to finance it. These serial entrepreneurs—unlike first-timers—know how to take short-cuts and be efficient. The current investment community also favors this approach, so this has been consecrated as the default startup model.

New entrepreneurs who employ this startup approach seldom recognize that the founder role extends beyond creating a new product and setting up a new company. Most don't know the question to ask and don't perform self-analysis to determine their competency for the founder role. Many are insecure about taking the helm so they have this default plan to improvise their founder / CEO / President role until they can afford to hire a qualified individual to take charge. In fact, many new founders find it easy and exciting to focus on developing their new business idea first; they believe that if their creation can sell and show promise, everything else will fall in place. This is like taking command of a vessel without having studied seamanship and planning resources for the long journey.

In addition, many fail to recognize new responsibilities and competencies that are needed as their company grows, and prepare for them. It's because most only focus on and prepare for the startup phase. Skills that are employed to set up a new business are different than skills required to build and manage a large team, solve budgetary crises, expand new sales channels, address changing consumer tastes and industry regulations, and so on.

Before you decide to devote most of your initial efforts and resources on product development, let me ask you to reflect on these scenarios. You wouldn't want to get on a plane without a qualified pilot, or on a train without a qualified conductor; nor would you want to embark on your entrepreneurial voyage if you are not a competent skipper.

As a new founder with a crew of two or a crew of 100, you shoulder immense responsibility and wield great influence over outcomes. You want to take the helm with confidence. A qualified captain possesses training and experience in survival skills, ship handling, maritime law, cargo operations, celestial navigation, and crew operations.

The Navigator will help you develop founder competency and navigate your entrepreneurial journey through different phases: startup, growth, expansion, and exit. The more qualified and prepared you are as captain, the better your journey and product will be.

What does it mean to be well prepared? Proper planning entails research, self-training, continual reflection, assessment, articulation, decision-making, and execution. You need to understand the big picture, key issues, and how to execute the details. In the frenzy of a startup, planning can avoid chaos and breakdown. This book will help you prepare so you can assume the helm confidently.

Who Should Read This Book

The Navigator is for aspiring founders of any age, race, gender, creed, background, or ability to learn. It's for anyone who contemplates starting his or her own business—whether profit or non-profit, whether it's a neighborhood shop owner, a service provider, a manufacturing firm, or a technology startup. This includes:

- Those who don't have time or money for entrepreneurial degree programs—professionals, breadwinners, working spouses, stay-at-home parents, single parents, veterans, and retirees.

- Seasoned professionals with deep expertise in their field but no experience in starting and running a new company.

- College / graduate students, as well as recent grads.

What You Can Achieve with This Book

An integrated mindset and approach will help you be strategic and tactical as you make decisions. An awareness of your responsibilities and skills required to take the helm confidently. An understanding of your importance and worth as founder, and how you can build your capacity throughout your venture. These will protect you and your creation.

Each founder is unique. What you bring on board and how you navigate will be unique. You shape your venture. You need to train and develop yourself into the most qualified captain that you can be. No one can do this for you. Only you can decide how well prepared you will be. How you start will affect how you perform—and how you end.

How to Use This Book

The Navigator is a guide to developing founder competency. Read this book through for an overview. Then re-read it more methodically. Questions and exercises will help you think through important issues that each new founder needs to address.

Use a notebook or a laptop to capture your answers while reading and working through exercises. Create your manifest with your answers and insights. Monitor the following and devise your action plan:

- Issues to reflect on and assess
- Skills you need to develop
- Resources you need to research and allocate
- Tools for your Survival Kit

You may find some exercises useful and others irrelevant, based on your experience. Skip areas you have mastered.

Some questions may be easy; others require effort to answer. Some may even raise more questions. Be patient. No need to be frustrated if you don't have answers. I've asked myself many questions over and over. Sometimes, it takes time to gain clarity.

Some questions may make you uncomfortable because they hit weak spots you've managed to avoid so far. Pay attention to those that make you want to say, "I dislike sales (or accounting or public relations)." When you find yourself thinking like this, recognize that your discomfort signals potential problems. Commit to addressing them before starting out or you may find them appearing during your venture.

Be honest regarding your abilities and limitations. Identify what you're willing to do. By knowing before you start, you can: 1) leverage personal and professional strengths, 2) monitor what you need to refine, 3) develop competency where needed, and 4) hire someone with competency or expertise to help you where you may be lacking.

Keep the following in mind. We absorb information and learn in our own way. Move at your own pace. The more time and energy you devote to your development now, the richer your self-discovery and preparation will be later on. New self-awareness and understanding will fortify you in your founder role. Insights gained from your own manifest will support you throughout your venture.

A clarification regarding definitions:

- **Venture** refers to the entirety of your entrepreneurial odyssey.

- **Startup** means a new entity that may be profit or nonprofit.

- **Product** means physical product, service, or software tool.

- **Operation** means: 1) a physical and/or virtual office; 2) marketing, sales, engineering, legal, and financial departments created to support your product and business; and 3) individuals who are responsible for various roles.

- **Infrastructure** refers to the framework (including business structures: research, marketing, sales, engineering, and legal), systems, and processes that support your operation.

The Path Not Taken

I wrote this book with the goal of helping you to move forward with your entrepreneurial journey. Moving forward means taking the next steps to prepare yourself as founder and skipper of your startup operation.

Moving forward can also mean that after reading this book and performing your due diligence, you conclude that you're not ready to leave your current job and life to start down a new career path this year, or that the entrepreneurial life is not for you. That's okay, too.

There's value in taking time to reacquaint yourself with your past and bring all that you are into the present. Furthermore, there's value in conducting self-examination and concluding that a path doesn't feel right because of an untenable product idea, lack of experience, resources, and/or consumer interest. Once you've gone through this initial process and obtained solid understanding of what's required to prepare and start well, you can be at peace with your decision to not go forward.

If you do decide to assume the helm as founder, allocate time to learn and grow in your new role.

Chapter I:
Employ a Framework to Develop as Founder

Your entrepreneurial journey is like a sea voyage with you as captain. As for a sea voyage, you'll want to be prepared for what you might encounter.

Plan Your Venture with an Integrated Mindset and Approach

Founder development starts with an integrated mindset, which views every individual, entity, and process as something whole made of integral parts.[1]

As an individual, we each belong to one or multiple communities. As founder, you're an integral part of a team and so are your crew members. Your product is a critical part of your new business, which will require an infrastructure to launch, operate, and grow.

An integrated mindset holds that all essential components of an entity or an operation should synchronize harmoniously and organically. In reality, integration seldom occurs accordingly. In particular, disorder is the norm within most startup operations. So, it is especially helpful to employ this mindset so you'll always recognize how essential moving parts fit into the big picture of your life, your founder role, your operation, and your journey.

A new founder is more likely to succeed if s/he embarks as an integrated individual; and a new business will have a higher chance of success if it's a well-integrated operation.

> *No man is an island, entire of itself.*
> *Every man is a piece of the continent, a part of the main.*
> John Donne

An Integrated Mindset

- The founder is an integrated individual
- The venture is an integrated entity

View the Founder as an Integrated Individual

As founder, you must determine what will be available for your journey. Begin with an understanding that we move through life each day with all that is in us: experiences, values, wisdom, instinct, habits, skills, dreams, goals, fears, successes, and failures. All of these factors affect decision-making. Each of us brings our whole self to each episode at home, play, or work. It's important to take stock of your life before starting a venture.

You'll need to integrate who you've been and what you've done with who you are and what you're doing. This will help you to know who you want to become and what you want to achieve. This includes identifying undeveloped parts of you that may be needed for future success.

You'll want to strive for an integrated state where mind, spirit, heart, and body are in good to excellent shape and working in concert to support and nourish you.

Develop and embark as an integrated individual and founder. Assess how your venture integrates into who you are. Begin a journey that will strengthen and affirm you. Advance your life path in a direction that feels right.

View the Venture as an Integrated Entity

Only a well-integrated engine will operate smoothly. A new venture requires time for planning, establishing standards, locating resources, acquiring talent, and setting a pace. You'll want to travel light, without unnecessary burdens. This means every material resource and every team member needs to fit well with your venture's purpose and core values.

Conversely, integration also occurs when the venture's purpose, values, brand identity, and standards permeate all aspects of your organization. This includes how you treat your employees and vendors, how you create and deliver your products, how your team communicates with your customers, how you obtain feedback, and how you build your company.

You'll want to think about how your business will integrate with your chosen industry. Will it align well with local and global markets, and the larger world? How will your product and entrepreneurial journey serve you, your family, and your community? How will the world be affected by your actions as founder? What positive or negative legacy are you creating?

Disruption has been a popular mantra for startups to embrace. Disruption can change outdated thinking and unhealthy habits. But not all disruption is good, especially disruption for its own sake. While your business idea may disrupt timeworn practices or monopolies, it can't exist in a disruptive mode. It needs stability of structure, standards, and processes. It needs to be a synchronized operation that moves forward seamlessly.

Employ an integrated mindset and avoid building your operation piecemeal. Otherwise, you'll find yourself back at the drawing board trying to create infrastructure, systems, and processes for something that's partially constructed.

When you have such a mindset, you'll always have a big picture view while you focus on the immediate priorities. You won't get caught in the trees and lost sight of the forest.

An Integrated Approach

An integrated approach takes account of what happens before you begin your venture. It includes the following important actions; these are listed sequentially. In reality, integration is not linear. Also, every individual is unique, so each may integrate differently.

Reflect
Reflect on your past. Bring clarity to your present and help prepare your future. Review and articulate what is yours: your intuition, wisdom, values, habits, winning approaches, successes, failures, challenges, powers, talents, skills, and life ambitions.

Assess
Evaluate all you uncovered during introspection. Decide what you want to jettison and what you're taking on your venture. Examine unresolved issues and questions newly emerged. Take note where you lack knowledge or competence.

Research
Research what you don't know. Prioritize issues and create an action plan to 1) refine or master needed skills, and 2) obtain resources you need to begin your venture.

Execute
Develop founder qualifications—whether by teaching yourself, taking classes, and/or working as an apprentice. Gather all that you bring to your venture, which include all intangible and material resources. Create your manifest and move forward.

An integrated mindset and approach will help you prepare well before starting out and keep you centered during your entrepreneurial journey so you won't lose sight of the big picture and the moving parts.

Understand Your Critical Role as Founder

As ship captain, you need to know what you're bringing on board in order to take the helm confidently. The most important thing you're bringing on board is you, not your product idea, which has no chance of success if you fail at the helm as skipper. The first step is to recognize and understand that you have the most critical role and shoulder immense responsibility.

- You're at the helm: you're in charge.
- You chart the course and set the pace.
- You have control over how you start your venture; the decisions you make before your trip can make or break it. You're responsible for everyone and everything you bring on board; gathering inadequate resources or choosing the wrong crew can affect your operation.
- You're responsible for strategic decisions that alter your future.
- When you encounter crises along the way, you're the one who resolves them.
- Your success depends on you.

First-time founders often commit two significant errors: 1) failing to realize the significance of their role, and 2) not preparing for it. Often they're so excited with their product that they devote all their energy and resources to product development first. This is like taking command of a vessel without having studied seamanship.

A qualified captain possesses training and experience in ship handling, maritime law, cargo operations, celestial navigation, and crew operations. Even if you lack the time or financial resources for formal training, this book will help you train yourself so that you develop competency and start well prepared.

Focus on Developing Founder Competency

Start by assessing how qualified you are in the founder role. If you lack skills, qualities, and training in certain areas, you'll need to develop basic competencies and hire those with needed skills and talents to support you. You don't need to be an expert in every function or role; you do need to acquire enough competence to ask the right questions for troubleshooting and problem resolution.

An important part of being competent is being self-reliant. When at sea, you have problems even when no other ship is in sight. Similarly, as you begin your venture, there will be crises, and no one will be available to help or else able to help because they aren't at the helm. You must be able to solve your own crises.

You won't have control over many factors in your venture, such as individuals or suppliers you hire, changes in markets, social or political currents, and emergence of new competitors or technologies. But you have control over you. You control what you know, what you're prepared to do, and what you're bringing aboard. You're the one who's always there for you. That's why self-reliance is essential.

Recognize Your Worth as Founder

Let's review the standard definition. Worth: usefulness or importance, as to the world, to a person, or for a purpose.[2]

Why is it important to know your worth? Knowing your worth helps you step forward from a position of strength. Everyone you want to enlist along the way—team members, strategic partners, investors, suppliers, and customers—will assess you as an individual and as founder. They'll assess your worth and your venture's worth. You need to know your worth and define it. If you don't, others will define it for you.

Many first-time founders rarely think about their own worth. With a product-centric mindset, they assign high value to founding their company and creating a product with potential. They believe this should give them significant negotiating leverage and control of their venture. But this isn't enough. Founders must create value beyond having developed product and starting a company. Investors who find a founder lacking won't hesitate to replace her.

As an individual, your sense of worth is based on how you perceive a variety of things—your value as a unique human being, character and qualities, family heritage, life experiences, accomplishments and failures, bank accounts, possessions, connections, and contributions to your community and the world. Your sense of worth may be influenced by your perception of how others see and value you. Most important, your worth is based on how you value yourself.

As founder, your worth includes all these factors, and you bring them with you on your venture. But your worth is also determined by past and future performances. How well you execute during your initial startup phase and later will magnify or diminish your worth.

Founder Insights

Reflect on the following, as you focus on augmenting your worth:
- As an individual, what do you have that is priceless to you?
- As an individual, what tangible and intangible assets do you bring to your founder's role?
- As founder, what do you hold in your possession and what will you develop to augment your worth and your venture's worth during your entrepreneurial journey?

You must have a clear sense of your worth as an individual and as a founder—and not just in monetary terms.

Knowing your worth is essential because:

- It empowers you to make decisions that serve and protect your interests and position.

- It gives you leverage when it comes to negotiating with new hires and new partnerships. You won't shortchange yourself with investors by giving away too much of your company for cash or other resources.

- It enables you to build on what you have (creating a product and starting a company) and magnify your worth (accomplishments in various roles beyond startup phase).

Focus on building your worth during your journey.

Envision Your Founder Role Throughout Your Venture's Life Cycle

Your venture has a preparation, a start, a middle, and an end. As founder, you are the main and constant factor. Think about how you will fulfill your responsibilities and increase your worth as you move through each phase.

Preparation Phase

Remember, "Proper planning prevents poor performance." Everything you do or don't do before starting will have direct and profound effects on your venture. Reflect and define what a great start means to you.

- Take stock of where you are so you know what you're bringing on board. Research which tools, skills, and resources you need to acquire. Develop founder competency.

- Outline what you hope to accomplish during your journey. Set goals and milestones as you move into each new phase.

Start Phase

Once you've started your voyage, you will know smooth sailing and rough waters. You'll need to overcome all kinds of challenges. You'll encounter developments over which you have no control. This include suppliers' price fluctuations, changing market trends, sudden resignation of a key team member, and/or new competitors. In addition to your founder role, you will need to perform other functional roles. What talents, skills, wisdom, and knowledge can you tap from within? Think about your various responsibilities and prepare yourself.

Growth Phase

As your venture gains momentum, you'll add new positions and team members. Your role as founder may change. How will you evolve in your role? What additional functional roles will you assume? What new skills do you need to acquire to expand your business? How can you increase your value, as you increase your contribution to the venture?

Exit Phase

If you decide to sell your business or step away, what skill sets do you need to help you position your company in an attractive light? How will buyers perceive your worth as founder? Will you be in such a strong position they'll court you for your business? Or will you get scant recognition and compensation for your role as founder?

Many first-time founders scarcely think about their skills and worth beyond their Start phase and treat the Growth and Exit Phases as something far down the road. They don't plan ahead. When they enter these phases, they find themselves unprepared and poorly positioned.

Keep in mind that each phase requires different skill sets. Monitor your own founder development and expanding responsibilities so you can develop relevant skills to help you succeed.

Recognize the Importance of Your Own Manifest

Every captain needs a manifest. Your manifest is more than a document that lists cargo, passengers, and crew. It contains your prep work and travel plan for your journey.

The exercises that you need to perform in this book constitute your prep work—reflection, assessment, research, and organization—all you will have done before starting your business. It will serve as your go-to resource when you need affirmation for why you started this journey. You're full of enthusiasm starting out. You may not feel you need a boost now, but you will.

I've witnessed high and low moments in founders. As a serial founder, I've lived these highs and lows. Highs add fuel to momentum; lows can be debilitating and paralyzing. There'll be rough days in your entrepreneurial journey, days when you ask why you embarked in the first place, moments when you doubt your judgment and wonder whether you possess smarts, skills, talent, and perseverance to succeed.

You're fortunate if you have a network of family, friends, and mentors to provide you with emotional support and be your cheerleaders. But they aren't living your founder's life; they can help only so far. Also, you'll experience crises when no one is around to call on, when everyone is occupied with their own priorities.

In today's round-the-clock connected world, many look outward for answers to problems. After all, "there's an app for everything." We rely on external sources to solve problems, whether internet searches, digital tools, crowd sourcing, and/or professional services. There'll be times when none of these will be accessible.

When you're at sea and have no backup, what will you have to help you? What can you rely on to save yourself and your venture? A founder needs to be as well qualified and prepared as can be. Since you can't plan for every crisis, you must be self-reliant.

So, while you're feeling energized, enthusiastic, and grounded, you'll want to create your own support system—with yourself as your Number One fan. You will be your go-to resource when you need to re-affirm faith in yourself and your venture.

The work that you do now, such as reflection, research, assessment, training, articulation, and organization—creating your manifest—will help you stock your Survival Kit so that you'll always be ready for emergencies and unanticipated disasters where help isn't available.

CHAPTER RECAP

Here's your framework for developing as a founder.

- Plan your venture with an integrated mindset and approach.

- Understand you have the most critical role and shoulder immense responsibility as founder.

- Recognize your need to develop competency before taking the helm.

- Acknowledge your worth as founder and focus on building it.

- Understand that each phase of your venture requires different skill sets. Take note of your expanding responsibilities and develop relevant skills for each phase to help you succeed.

- Monitor your founder development and protect your worth throughout your entrepreneurial journey.

Create your own manifest, which will prove essential on your journey as your field guide and go-to resource. It will remind you why you undertook it—and how you're going to succeed.

Chapter II:
Invest in Yourself

Refine the self and set up the foundation.
Chang Po-Tuan (Translated by Thomas Cleary)

Once you begin, you'll be thinking, doing, and living your venture 24/7. It will require all you've got. You must be clear about all you bring to it.

When asked, "What do you bring to the table?" aspiring founders often point to their resumes and list operational expertise, industry experience, professional networks, and sometimes personal assets. When probed further, it becomes clear that most haven't thought much beyond these areas.

As founder, you bring more than just operational and industry experience. You bring your life's experiences with you wherever you go. Your instinct, wisdom, attitudes, values, habits, successes, failures, strengths, weaknesses, hopes, and fears influence your decision-making process every day. You will bring all this, all of you to your venture. All that you are will affect how you plan, execute, and respond to challenges. All that you are will determine how you interact with others, including under stress.

Before you move forward, take time for introspection and self-examination. Get updated on who you are. Be integrated in mind, body, heart, and spirit before taking on your new role. Failure to delve deeply in advance is frequent among first-time founders. Yet you need to understand what you, specifically, are bringing to your venture.

First, take a snapshot of where you are today. Below are questions to get you started. Don't spend too much time on it. If you find yourself struggling to articulate an answer, leave the question unanswered for now and move on. When done, move to the next section. Return to unanswered questions later, after you've reflected on them.

Exercise 1: A Snapshot of Where You Are Today

1. Articulate what you love about your life.

Where You Are Today		
Area	What you love about your life	What you are doing to maintain or refine
Personal • Mind • Body • Spirit • Heart • Finance		
Home (Family)		
Work		
Community		

2. What is your center of gravity? Who or what grounds you as you move through daily life? Your grandmother, parents, best friend, children, partner, heritage?

3. What are your daily sources of stress? What are your recurrent challenges?

	Recurrent Challenges	
Area	What are your daily sources of stress	How you manage or minimize them
Personal • Mind • Body • Spirit • Heart • Finance		
Home (Family)		
Work		
Community		

4. What are the three most important decisions you ever made?

Most Important Decisions		
Decision	Result: success or failure	Lesson learned
1.		
2.		
3.		

5. What are your lifelong aspirations? Are you living and working toward them? If not, what is hindering you, and what do you think is the cause? What can you do to get to closer to realizing your aspirations?

6. How do you envision living your life where everything is deeply aligned?

A Life Aligned		
Area	Ideal condition and situation	Actions you are taking to achieve it
Personal • Mind • Body • Spirit • Heart • Finance		
Home (Family)		
Work		
Community		

7. What are your priorities and goals for this year? For next year?

8. What are the top three reasons you want to leave your current situation?

9. Why do you want to start a new business? Before you answer this question, know that you might be having two conversations: a) what you're telling the world, and b) what you're telling yourself.

10. Why is your new business idea so compelling to you? Is this a must-do?

11. Why not work for an established company that offers a similar service or product?

12. How will your new entrepreneurial life align with your lifelong aspirations?

13. How do you think this new business will transform your life?

14. How will your product or service contribute to the world?

15. What are you willing to sacrifice to pursue this venture?

16. What will happen and how will you feel if you don't pursue it?

Make Time for Introspection

He that will not reflect is a ruined man.
Japanese proverb

The most important exercise that an aspiring founder can perform is introspection. It isn't the first thing that comes to mind for one who's excited about her product idea and contemplating a new venture. Yet it's crucial because while your business idea may evolve or change completely, the one constant that you want and need is a qualified and dependable skipper at the helm.

As founder, the one person whom you can rely on 24/7 is you. You want to be as competent, as well prepared as you can be. Start by allocating time to reflect and take stock of who you are, where you've been, where your life is, and what you're bringing on board to navigate your entrepreneurial voyage successfully.

Introspection is a gift you give yourself. If you're a reflective individual, then you have a head start. If you're one of those individuals who find it difficult to sit still, recognize that making time to be quiet and focus inward is a learned behavior. We can't hear our thoughts or feel our emotions, or become aware of our inner riches if we're distracted by round-the-clock news, to-dos, messaging apps, music, videos, the outrage of the week, and crowds. If you can turn off your digital life for a few hours or a Saturday and be still, you'll see things you overlooked in your hurried pace. There is value in doing nothing, but you won't recognize it if you're in constant motion.

Introspection enhances self-awareness. In silence and stillness, reflect on your life and how they inform who you are. Articulate what all of you means and visualize how you want to evolve, what you want to accomplish. Introspection helps you understand why you make certain decisions. It can prevent bad decisions as much as inform good decisions. It helps you to recognize your strengths and areas you need to fortify. You'll start noticing blind spots and you'll become aware of habits that you've taken for granted; some have served you well and some you might want to jettison. Your personal riches will reveal themselves to you—if you give yourself time to uncover them.

In addition, introspection gives you a better understanding of others and the world around us. There is truth to the old adage that, "The answer lies within."

Yet, introspection isn't a priority because we juggle personal, familial, and professional demands, along with "maintenance tasks" of life in the 21st-century: fill the gas tank, pay bills, buy groceries, do laundry, and attend to children and parents. Introspection is eclipsed when held hostage by the Immediacy Mindset. We're under continuous pressure to do everything now. We scurry from one task or event to another. Shifting priorities and media onslaught keep us distracted. For most, life is a flurry of hurries.

For so many, we have no incentive to employ reflection as a tool for growth, solving problems, and clarifying what we think we know, want, and/or need. This is because we live bombarded by marketing messages that poke us on how we should live, what we should own, how to dress, what to eat, how to raise children, how and when to retire, and what drugs we'll need when we do. It's easy to avoid introspection, when answers can be found instantly on search engines or in headlines. And, "there's always an app for that."

We further undervalue introspection because being still and quiet makes us uncomfortable. We live in a society that encourages action and not repose. We don't make time for it, unless illness forces us to sit still or we hit a relationship crisis or a career roadblock. Even those who can afford time for thought find it challenging to be still and reflect deeply. For some, introspection is scary. It deals with issues we've long ignored. But if you have the courage to take the entrepreneurial path, you'll be able to tap that same courage to face issues thoughtfully.

Begin your introspection by reviewing and assessing several areas to articulate who you are and what makes you tick. This will help you integrate your past with your present and future.

- Identify Your Sources of Influence
- Assess Your Habits
- Review Your Accomplishments
- Analyze Your Failures
- Examine Your Window of Beliefs
- Uncover Your Sources of Power

Identify Your Sources of Influence

Start by identifying influences in your life. Most of us know what these are, but few take time to articulate or probe them. We forget how much we're influenced by individuals, family, places, and past experiences, until forced by some crisis to turn inward for understanding and solutions.

Influencing sources may inspire or inhibit you. They color your values and prejudices; these will be reflected in your venture. They even affect your attitudes toward time management and human relations or how you spend money and resources. Your "sources of influence" affects your decision-making as a person and in your role as founder.

The more aware you are of what and who influences you, the more you'll understand why you act as you do, why you avoid certain things. And the more you understand, the more power and control you'll have over how you choose to respond to encounters on your journey.

Introspection will reveal insights and tools that you'll need. It includes blind spots and unexamined assumptions that you've held for a long time. Be courageous and open to new revelations.

Exercise 2: Sources of Influence

Family

The adage "The apple doesn't fall far from the tree" is true. Our parents and relatives are our first sources of influence. Think about your family's history. Here are some questions that may help you reflect.

Identify Sources. What are family traditions or stories that have stayed with you? What are your grandparents' and parents' attitudes toward life, family, work, and play? Do they see life as a glass half full or half empty? What did they each prize the most? What standards or ideals did they try to uphold? What were their priorities?

Articulate. Think of three things that you've inherited from your family, which have shaped your beliefs, values, and daily conduct—negatively or positively. Who influenced you the most?

Family		
Tradition / Value / Habit / Attitude / Lesson learned	Positive or negative influence	How this source appears in your daily life
1.		
2.		
3.		

Friends

After parents, friends wield the most influence over many of us. We look to them for emotional support, as well as input on romantic interests, fashion choices, entertainment options, and career decisions.

Identify Sources. Which friends have influenced you the most?

Articulate. Think of three things that you've learned from friends, which have shaped your attitudes and behavior—negatively or positively.

Friends		
Tradition / Value / Habit / Attitude / Lesson learned	Positive or negative influence	How this source appears in your daily life
1.		
2.		
3.		

Role Models and Archetypes

Some have role models who aren't family or friends. Archetypes are personalities that appear in mythologies and folklores around the world. Archetypes include Hero, Warrior, Crusader, Explorer, Caregiver, Helper, Rebel, Revolutionary, Creator, Inventor, Scholar, Philosopher, Researcher, Thinker, Teacher, Builder, Catalyst, Visionary, and Leader. We encounter them in books, movies, and daily life. They lurk in our psyches and influence us.

For example, a schoolmate attended a talk by the Tibetan Buddhist Pema Chödrön and decided to become a monk. A friend—inspired by the medieval village's healer and herbalist—became a physician.

Identify Sources. What role models and archetypes influence and inspire you, other than family and friends? Why do they inspire you deeply?

Articulate. Think of three things that you've integrated into your daily life from your role models and archetypes.

Role Models and Archetypes		
Tradition / Value / Habit / Attitude / Lesson learned	Positive or negative influence	How this source appears in your daily life
1.		
2.		
3.		

School

We spent much of our growing years away from home in school.

Identify Sources. Who at school—teachers, coaches, counselors, and classmates—have left indelible marks on you?

Articulate. Think of three insights, approaches, or processes that you learned from those who taught and coached you. Include both healthy and unhealthy habits.

School		
Tradition / Value / Habit / Attitude / Lesson learned	Positive or negative influence	How this source appears in your daily life
1.		
2.		
3.		

Work

Work is where we spent much of our adult life. For many, work is a continuing education.

Identify Sources. What have you learned from your supervisors, peers, direct reports, vendors, and/or suppliers?

Articulate. Think of three insights, approaches, or processes that you picked up from your work life. Include healthy or unhealthy habits.

Work		
Tradition / Value / Habit / Attitude / Lesson learned	Positive or negative influence	How this source appears in your daily life
1.		
2.		
3.		

Environment

Our physical, cultural, and social environments affect our mental, emotional, and physical states. As you think about building a new environment, review how different environments affected you.

Identify Sources. Physical environments. Where did you grow up? Was it urban, suburban, or rural? Was it a wealthy or poor neighborhood? Was your family affluent or struggling? Did your family move around a lot or did you live in the same house until you went off to college?

Cultural/Social environments. Did you grow up in a religious, agnostic, or atheistic environment? Did you live in a homogeneous or multicultural neighborhood?

Articulate. Think about three insights you've culled from living, working, and interacting in different environments. How have they influenced your personal and professional decisions?

Environment		
Tradition / Value / Habit / Attitude / Lesson learned	Positive or negative influence	How this source appears in your daily life
1.		
2.		
3.		

Now that you've thought about various sources of influence, over the next few weeks, think about how they may affect you as founder.

Assess Your Habits

We each carry a lifetime of acquired habits—from our parents, friends, teachers, colleagues, partners, and peers. Some were acquired by choice or fancy; others by necessity—for work, health reasons, or survival.

We wake up each day to navigate through a routine that includes home, family, work, and community. Punctuality, responsiveness, and resourcefulness are some "habitual tools" we employ to move through each day. Mostly, we don't give much thought to these tools because they're second nature. We become aware of them when a mishap occurs, or when someone points them out.

As founder, be aware of your habits, which will give you insight into habits of others. Reinforce good ones and bring them on board; jettison bad ones. Assess your habits.

- General Habits
- Mental Habits
- Work Habits
- Financial Habits
- Wellness Habits

General Habits

Most of us rely heavily on daily habits without taking time to assess them. Evaluate the following eight habits.

Exercise 3: General Habits

General Habits	
Habit	Rate where you are with each habit (1 = abysmal; 2 = competent; 3 = strong; 4 = excellent). Decide an action for growth if you see room for improvement
1. Punctuality (Strict observance in keeping engagements; promptness)	
2. Responsiveness (The act of responding readily to appeals, efforts, influences, etc.)	
3. Responsibility (The state of being answerable or accountable for something within one's power, control, or management)	
4. Diligence (Constant and earnest effort to accomplish what is under taken)	
5. Trustworthiness (The state of deserving of trust or confidence; dependability; reliability)	
6. Collaboration (Working with others)	

General Habits	
Habit	Rate where you are with each habit (1 = abysmal; 2 = competent; 3 = strong; 4 = excellent). Decide an action for growth if you see room for improvement
7. Resourcefulness (Ability to deal skillfully and promptly with new situations, difficulties; problem solving)	
8. Integrity (Adherence to moral and ethical principles; honesty)	

Mental Habits

Understanding how you learn helps you be more aware of where you're strong and what you need to strengthen. It also helps you be more aware of how others learn. This will ultimately help you become a better founder, manager, student, mentor, and collaborator.

Exercise 4: Method of Learning

How You Learn		
Method	Rank them in the order of most preferred (1) to least preferred (5) method	Assess and note what works well for you and where you want to improve
1. Reading		
2. Listening		
3. Watching a tutorial, a demonstration, or observing a behavior		

How You Learn		
Method	Rank them in the order of most preferred (1) to least preferred (5) method	Assess and note what works well for you and where you want to improve
4. Discussing with others; collaborating		
5. Doing or testing (trial and error)		

Exercise 5: Time of Day You Learn Best

Some absorb new information or techniques in the morning. Others don't become alert until the evening. When is the best time for you to learn? If you haven't paid attention to this, you'll want to develop awareness of it to improve your learning habits. Knowing when you best learn or study can help you plan time more effectively.

When You Learn Best	
Time of day	Rank your most effective (1) to least effective time period (7)
Early morning	
Late morning	
Noon time	
Early afternoon	
Early evening	
Late evening	
After midnight	

Exercise 6: Settings Where You Learn Most Effectively

Ideal Condition for Learning	
Setting	Rank your most effective (1) to least effective setting (5)
1. By yourself, in silence	
2. By yourself, with background music or noise	
3. In group setting (classroom, workshops, library, or coffee shop)	
4. In a corporate setting (open floor plan, cubicle, or private office)	
5. Other	

If you're going from an office job with many colleagues to your own home office, how will you adjust to this change? What environment and conditions will you create?

Exercise 7: Thinking Habits

We rely on our minds to work for us without taking the time to reflect on how we process information, observations, and insights. How we think affects how we act, decide, or refrain from deciding. Review what you take for granted each day.

How do you think? Examine your thinking style and enhance your awareness of how others think. Below are descriptions of different types of thinkers. These are a few profiles to help you reflect on your thinking process. No one is a "purist" thinker. You may find yourself possessing a combination of thinking styles, with some more dominant than others.

How You Think	
Profile and Characteristics	Rate yourself (1 = least like me; 2 = somewhat; 3 = strongly; 4 = most like me)
1. The realist / pragmatist • Recognizes the constraints and uses what is available. • Blind spot: may be too pragmatic and less willing to consider creative or unconventional solutions.	
2. The idealist • Strives for higher standards and ideals. • Blind spot: may wait for ideal conditions and ignore problems that need to be resolved immediately.	
3. The strategist • Approaches the journey or problem with a big picture and long-term perspective. • Blind spot: may miss the finer details and immediate issues that need attention and resolution.	
4. The tactician • Focuses on solving current challenges; executes with precision and thoroughness. • Blind spot: may miss the view of the big picture.	

How You Think	
Profile and Characteristics	Rate yourself (1 = least like me; 2 = somewhat; 3 = strongly; 4 = most like me)
5. The eclectic • Is open to all kinds of ideas, perspectives, and resources; solves problems with a unique / unconventional approach. • Blind spot: may juggle too many factors and lack focus.	
6. The purist • Makes decisions based on what s/he was taught as effective; doesn't deviate from time-honored practices. • Blind spot: may be too rigid when problem solving requires flexibility and compromise.	

Knowing about the different styles of thinking can help you refine your own style and become more aware of how future employees, business partners, and suppliers think, and if their styles align or conflict with yours. Note that diversity is a plus to discerning emerging problems. If you surround with those who share your style, you'll likely miss out on new perspectives and potential solutions during critical moments.

In addition to this exercise, read books on thinking styles to develop deeper self-awareness.

Exercise 8: Decision-making Habits

We make small to big decisions every day. Our backgrounds, genetic talents, skills, and personal wisdom shape our decision-making habits.

As founder, you'll be on the spot for strategic and tactical decisions. Understand how you make decisions, and note how those around you make decisions. When you understand and trust the decision-making process of employees and colleagues, you can delegate easily. You communicate and negotiate with more clarity and efficiency. For a week or two, observe how you make decisions.

Situation 1: When it comes to what to wear, what to eat, what daily tasks to prioritize, how do you describe your decision-making habit?

Situation 2: When it comes to big decisions (like where to attend university, what career path to pursue, when to change jobs, when to make a big purchase, or who to marry), how do you describe your decision-making habit?

Situation 3: Think of personal, familial, and professional crises you have encountered, where your decision was needed. How do you describe your decision-making habit?

How You Decide	
Profile and characteristics	Rate yourself (1 = least like me; 2 = somewhat; 3 = strongly; 4 = most like me)
Decisive • You review only information that is available to you. You conduct no additional research, consider the pros and cons, and decide quickly. • Blind spot: not recognizing that some decisions require waiting for additional information and deliberation.	

How You Decide	
Profile and characteristics	Rate yourself (1 = least like me; 2 = somewhat; 3 = strongly; 4 = most like me)
Thoughtful and measured • You research extensively all options, consider the pros and cons, and then decide. You cannot be pressed into a hurried decision. • Blind spot: not recognizing that sometimes you cannot afford the time for in-depth research.	
Procrastinating • You avoid researching and making decisions until the last minute. • Blind spot: lack of research and attention to time-sensitive issues can lead to loss of opportunity, crisis or failure.	

Clearly, different situations call for different decision-making processes. Assess and decide what works well for you and where you need to refine.

In addition to this exercise, read books on decision-making styles and cognitive biases to develop deeper self-awareness.

Work Habits

As founder, you create a working environment most suitable to you. It's important to understand how you work so you can optimize time and resources. You'll need to understand each new team member's work style, and how that fits into your venture. This will help you identify opportunities for synergy. New companies often run into glitches because founders didn't set up working criteria for team members to observe. When there are no definitions, standards, and processes in place, chaos occurs. When people don't know what's expected, miscommunication occurs.

Most of us adapt to corporate structures of our jobs. We took them for granted and have not reflected on our own working standards, rhythms, productivity patterns, and preferred environments. Now is a good time to assess how you work.

Exercise 9: Work Standards

On the personal and professional levels, we hold ourselves to certain ethical, moral, and performance standards. To one individual, this means punctuality. To another, it means dedicated workspace and an organized schedule. To another, it means exceeding expectations and always delivering a bit more to clients than promised. Review and assess.

Work Standards	
What daily work standards and habits do you have in place for yourself? Articulate three that have served you well.	
What are your recurrent challenges? What's the one task that can help you improve?	
New practice(s) that you would like to add in your founder role.	

Exercise 10: Work Rhythm

Most of us must live by a corporate working schedule of 8-to-6. Yet most of us have never taken time to discover if this routine suits us; some aren't aware of circadian rhythms, their working rhythm, or productivity pattern.

Alan Lakein, an expert on personal time management, wrote about Prime Time in his book, *How to Get Control of Your Time and Your Life.*[3] Internal Time is when you work best—morning, afternoon, or evening. External Prime Time is the best time to attend to other people—those you have to deal with in your job, intramural sports, volunteer work, and so on. Review and assess.

Work Rhythm	
What are your internal and external prime times? Are you a night owl or a morning person?	
How would you describe natural working rhythm? For example: work straight for hours without break, or work with needed breaks.	
If you are aware of your internal and external prime times, how have you made them work for you?	
What are your recurrent challenges? What's one task that can help you optimize your work rhythm?	

Exercise 11: Productivity Pattern

You may know about the 80/20 rule. The Italian economist Vilfredo Pareto came up with this formula, which holds true across many disciplines and industries: 80% of results come from 20% of efforts; 80% of sales come from 20% of products; 80% of revenues come from the top 20% customers.[4] Review and assess.

Productivity Pattern	
Think about your life at home and at work. What are key drivers that affect your daily productivity level?	
How would you describe your daily productivity level? Are you an 80/20? A 50/50, a 70/30, or a 90/10?	
What is your optimal productivity ratio and are you achieving it frequently / steadily?	
Implement one or two tasks to improve your productivity level.	

Exercise 12: Work Environment

As founder, you get to create your work environment. Review all your prior work environments as well as the work you did under Work Habits section. Take note of what has worked well for you and what needs to change.

Work Environment	
Are you most productive working in a closed-door office or in an open-floor plan?	
Do you need white noise or background noise in order to be productive?	
Do you work best alone or around people?	
What is your ideal work environment?	

Think about your preferred work habits and changes you can make to improve them. List all your criteria and prioritize your must-haves.

Financial Habits

Review and assess your attitude toward money and how these affect your financial habits before you start your new venture. You want to leverage strengths and identify habits you may need to monitor or improve.

Exercise 13: Financial Habits

Ask yourself the questions below. Reflect carefully about your financial habits, and project how you will spend and save as a founder.

1. Describe your attitude toward money. Do you view it as a positive resource or a stressful necessity?

2. Do you love numbers? Are you good with accounting? Or do you avoid dealing with numbers?

3. Is money something that comes easily for you or do you worry about it all the time?

4. Do you enjoy making money? Spending it? Saving it? Hoarding it?

5. Are you known as someone who is parsimonious, frugal, cautious, or spendthrift?

6. Where does the money you make go?
    *   Personal (appearance, fitness, recreation) _____
    *   Family / Home _____
    *   Work _____
    *   Savings _____
    *   Other _____

7. How would you describe your financial habits?
   • Dismal and needing an overhaul _____
   • Juggling with room for improvement _____
   • Sensible with occasional indulgences _____
   • Disciplined _____

8. What positive habits should you keep and which ones should you monitor, improve, or jettison?

Startup Anecdotes

Most first-time entrepreneurs rarely review financial habits before starting ventures. One corporate lawyer-turned-entrepreneur spent like he was still working in his swanky law firm, when he should have been bootstrapping.

I worked with a few founders who were careless when it came to investors' money; they wrongly believed that because they'd been successful in raising money the first round, there was more to come. Consequently, they didn't budget or bootstrap. They went on a hiring binge and splurged on office space and equipment. Before acquiring enough paying customers to cover overhead costs, they ran out of money and had to shut down.

Other founders were so tight with money that while they expected best service and performance from others, they weren't willing to pay for it.

If you're someone who spends liberally, monitor your habit and be cautious with your startup's budget. If you're someone who count pennies, beware that cutting corners at the start may create operational problems later. For example, not paying people what they're worth led to resentment, poor performance, and high turnover.

Your attitude toward money and your financial habits can help build your venture, or lead to a shutdown.

Wellness Habits

Starting a company is exciting; it's also stressful. I've known founders who were in excellent health when they started out. Within a year, they gained weight, suffered insomnia, and developed high blood pressure. One founder's dormant asthma reappeared; another developed digestive issues. They claimed they didn't have time to exercise.

Exercise 14: Wellness Habits

Wellness Habits		
Area	Rate your wellness status (1 = poor; 2 = average; 3 = good; 4 = excellent). What helps you stay fit	Action that is needed to maintain or improve your wellness status
Mind		
Body		
Spirit		
Heart		

You need to assume that your journey is a long voyage instead of a sprint. Your wellness is important because you need strength and endurance. You need to be in good to excellent health. This means eating right, getting enough sleep, exercising, making time to clear your mind and spirit, and resolving emotional conflicts. You need to decompress from daily stress and recharge. If you don't, you will find yourself beset with physical, emotional, and mental health issues. This, in turn, will affect your performance as founder and your startup's well-being.

Review Your Accomplishments

Think about how your accomplishments and lessons learned may influence you in your founder role.

Exercise 15: Best Decisions

Review the best decisions you've made in life, such as deciding where to attend college, when to take your first solo adventure, skill sets you decided to learn, first internship you took, whom you married, and where you chose to live. A great decision can mean deciding against something—not to move, not to take a job, and so on.

Best Decisions			
Decision	Situation / Condition	Instinct / Skill / Talent / Tool you employed	How decision affected your life
1.			
2.			
3.			

Exercise 16: Best Form

Think about the times when you were at the top of your game. What factors or qualities enabled you to be in top form?

Best Form			
Instant when you were at top of your game	Situation / Condition	Instinct / Skill / Talent / Tool you employed	How each affected your life
1.			
2.			
3.			

Exercise 17: Winning Approach

Some individuals have developed a tried-and-true formula for accomplishing a fitness goal, a financial goal, or a career goal. Do you have a winning approach? What are your recurrent successes?

Winning Approach			
Action / Pattern of success	Situation / Condition	Instinct / Skill / Talent / Tool you employed	How this affected your life
1.			
2.			
3.			

Exercise 18: Challenges Overcome

Think about the most difficult challenges that you have encountered and how you overcame them successfully.

Challenges Overcome			
Challenge resolved successfully	Situation / Condition	Instinct / Skill / Talent / Tool you employed	How this affected your life
1.			
2.			
3.			

Analyze Your Failures

Exercise 19: Worst Decisions

We've all made huge blunders at one time or another. Own and analyze your missteps so you will remember what to avoid, what to monitor.

Worst Decisions			
Biggest blunder you've committed	Situation / Condition	Instinct / Skill / Talent / Tool you should have employed	How this affected your life
1.			
2.			
3.			

Exercise 20: Recurrent Challenges

We all have issues that we struggle with time and again. These may include not listening well, not taking a stand, avoiding confrontation, overcommitting, always running late, or overspending. As you're taking stock of your tools for your venture, acknowledge these challenges and address them.

Recurrent Challenges			
Recurrent challenge	Recurrent pattern of response	How this has affected your life	Skill / Talent / Tool / Action / Attitude that may resolve
1.			
2.			
3.			

Exercise 21: Hot Buttons

We all possess sensitive areas where an event or a comment may trigger the nasty beast within. Acknowledge your hot button issues. Learn how to self-manage so you can minimize or avoid situations that may trigger them.

Hot Buttons			
Issue	Recurrent pattern of response	How this has affected your life	Skill / Talent / Tool / Action / Attitude that may resolve
1.			
2.			
3.			

Examine Your Window of Beliefs

We each view the world through a unique window of beliefs about life, time, money, family, friends, and work. This is the result of experiences and various sources of influence. Our beliefs affect attitudes, which affect our actions. Next is an exercise to help you examine your beliefs.

Example: Sam's Window of Beliefs and How It Rules Sam	
Belief	Action reflecting belief
• I am an optimist. I see life as a glass half full. I view life as a journey with ups and downs, twists and turns.	• I always choose to focus on the upside and solve problems from this perspective.
• I believe everyone has something to contribute.	• I try to consider an individual's opinion or position before rejecting or accepting it.
• I value Time and see it as a resource, not as an adversary.	• I am always punctual because I respect my time and show others I respect theirs.

When you have insight into your own beliefs, you'll have insight into how others see the world and why they act as they do. You'll become aware of those who share similar beliefs and those who differ from you.

Exercise 22: Window of Beliefs

How Your Beliefs Rule You	
1. Belief about life	Action reflecting belief
2. Belief about self	Action reflecting belief
3. Belief about family	Action reflecting belief
4. Belief about work	Action reflecting belief
5. Belief about play	Action reflecting belief
6. Belief about rest	Action reflecting belief
7 Belief about time	Action reflecting belief
8. Belief about money	Action reflecting belief
9. Belief about people	Action reflecting belief

In the next few weeks, give yourself time to think about how your beliefs will affect your actions as founder.

Uncover Your Sources of Power

> *The most common way people give up their power*
> *is by thinking they don't have any.*
> Alice Walker

Each day, we wield all kinds of power, but seldom analyze it. Before starting your venture, reflect on what powers you possess so you know what you can access.

The standard definition for power is the ability to do or act.[5] This includes acting physically, mentally, emotionally, legally, morally, financially, technically, and artistically. Power that you exert over yourself can be thought of as agency, self-management, self-discipline, or self-mastery. Power that you exert over others may be viewed as clout—ability to influence someone's thinking and actions.

Do you know your sources of power? How well do you wield them? Here's one way of viewing and uncovering your powers.

Internal Sources of Power

Your internal sources of power are those that you access from within, any time, anywhere. They are available in the following realms:

- Mental – Analytical, technical, intellectual, problem solving skills, and curiosity.
- Spiritual – Faith in whatever inspires, grounds, and nurtures you.
- Emotional – Ability to manage your emotions, connect with and relate to others, express, and exercise restraint when appropriate.
- Physical – How you appear, present yourself, and communicate.

You also have your intuition and wisdom at your disposal. We often take these qualities for granted and don't give much weight to them as sources of power. Most of us don't even acknowledge to ourselves that we possess wisdom; it's not in vogue in today's culture, which fixates on power that's tangible and measurable.

You can access your mental faculties, emotional temperament, spiritual foundation, and physical well-being at any time. Cultivate them. Nurture them so they can serve you at any moment.

External Sources of Power

Your external sources of power may include:

- Reputation / personal brand
- Money
- Assets – Material possessions, intellectual property, etc.
- Position – Your standing within your company, your industry niche, your community, and organizations where you are a formal or informal member.

External sources of power can enhance personal clout and expand spheres of influence. But you may not always have access to external sources of power. Use them to prepare and build your business, but tap what is accessible to you 24/7.

Startup Anecdotes

An engineer founded a company and assumed three positions: founder, CTO, and CEO. Ken was insecure about his CEO responsibilities and powers from the start. He was most comfortable with technical skills so he often hid in his CTO office. He surfaced to deal with team management, business development, and operations—when pressed for a decision as Founder-CEO.

His startup moved along, but never took off at full steam because Ken was seldom at the helm. After four years, tired of his CEO duties, Ken sold his business to a competitor who shut it down.

•••

An individual named Jess and her spouse bankrolled a new business. They both took the title "Co-Founder" and decided that Jess would assume the CEO position during early years. Jess struggled as CEO because she found the accompanying powers and responsibilities overwhelming. While Jess excelled at product and market research, she acknowledged that she chafed when she had to exercise her CEO powers, like firing incompetent engineers, developing new clients, and negotiating new deals. This reluctance led her to neglect one of her main duties, which was to lead her team members during a critical time that required her presence. Because she wasn't at the helm, her crew deserted, and the venture stalled.

Many first-time founders assume the CEO role without spending time researching and reflecting on what it means to wear the CEO hat—perform required duties and wield accompanying powers. Many assume this role completely unprepared. This is a common blind spot and an understandable one.

Founder Insights

On a daily basis, most of us don't spend time thinking about our powers. Instead we give them away because we're taught to look outward for power, money, possessions, and status. We endow holders of these with power.

We're not taught to recognize innate resources that we can develop and use to magnify our power. Knowing what your internal powers are and when to tap them empowers. When self-aware and self-possessed, you invoke recognition for your internal powers.

You have the power:
- To say, "Yes," but only when you are ready and confident with your decision.
- To say, "No" to an offer that doesn't work for you.
- Not to shortchange yourself or undervalue your business.
- To ask for more—because you believe in what you're offering.

As a self-reliant and prepared founder, you'll need all your powers.

Exercise 23: Sources of Power

Internal Sources of Power		
Internal power	How and when do you wield this power	How do you rate this power? (1 = weak, 2 = competent, 3 = strong, 4 = excellent / second nature)
Mental		
Spiritual		
Emotional		
Physical		

External Sources of Power		
External power	How and when do you wield this power	How do you rate this power? (1 = weak; 2 competent; 3 = strong; 4 = excellent / second nature)
Reputation / Personal brand		
Money		
Assets		
Position (social, professional, and community)		

Reflect on all your powers. How often do you tap them? Which have served you well? Which do you want to strengthen? Think about how you will carry your powers into your venture, and how you will deploy and exercise them.

From Introspection to Integration

Now that you've spent time reflecting and assessing, you should have a better understanding of how you allocate time, where you're most effective, and where you need to improve. You should have more clarity regarding how your past has influenced you, where and who you are in your present, and what you can take with you on your venture.

Your Introspection time should give you more clarity regarding the following issues; these should be articulated and addressed before stepping into your new role. Be patient if you don't have an immediate or clear answer; sometimes it takes a while before clarity appears.

State Your Purpose

Exercise 24: Purpose

1. What is your life's purpose? How is your purpose reflected in your daily life, in your personal life, and in your work life?

2. What are your current life's priorities? What are your daily and weekly priorities? Do they reflect your purpose? What action plan do you have in place to ensure you are achieving your purpose and honoring those priorities?

3. What have you accomplished? Are you meeting your short-term and long-term goals? What else do you want to realize?

4. What is your personal brand? If someone had to describe your brand, what would you like to hear her say? What do you do to build it, maintain it, and refine it?

5. What kind of legacy do you want to create?

Articulate Your Core Values

Exercise 25: Core Values

What are your core values? How are they present in your personal as well as professional life?

Core Values	
Value	Daily action that reflects value
1.	
2.	
3.	

Know Your Main Influencers

Now that you've spent time examining your past and reacquainting yourself with sources of influence, prioritize the top three that affect your daily outlook and inform your decision-making. It's important to know who and what inspires or what hinders you, because this will influence your actions as founder.

Exercise 26: Main Influencers

Top Sources of Influence	
Sources of influence that affects you positively	Sources of influence that you need to jettison
1.	
2.	
3.	

Acknowledge What Drives You

Exercise 27: Motivation

1. What drives you to take action, to accomplish all that you have thus far in your life?

2. What compels you to embark on this entrepreneurial path? This is the first question I often ask of new founders.

You may be having two conversations. The first is what you're telling the world about why you're starting a new business, and the second is what you're telling yourself.

Give yourself time to mull over the questions. Write down the answer. Look at it often. Revise. If you find yourself struggling for an answer, you need to dig deeper. Revise until you have a concise answer that reflects your true motivation. If you can't find your true conviction, you may find yourself faltering during crises.

Here are answers given by past founders:
- "Realize my dream of running my own business by leveraging my passion and talents."
- "Work for myself and not for a corporation."
- "Obtain more flexibility in my work routine for family reasons."
- "Have more creative freedom."
- "Obtain financial independence."
- "Create a new service or a new product because a family member needs it, and there's no such product in the market."
- "I see a problem I am compelled to solve."

Note Your Habits

Previously, you've spent some time reviewing and assessing various habits. Prioritize the top three that serve you well and those that you need to monitor or let go.

Exercise 28: Habits

Habits	
Habit you that serve you well	Habit that you need to monitor or jettison
1.	
2.	
3.	

Evaluate Your Work-in-Progress

Introspection should have shed some light into areas in need of improvement: your work-in-progress. Before you begin a new chapter, articulate those you need to address.

Exercise 29: Work-in-Progress

Work-in-Progress	
Area	Issue to address and how they may affect your founder role
Personal • Mind • Body • Spirit • Heart • Finance	
Home (Family)	
Work	
Community	

Adopt a "Wholistic" and Integrated Mindset

Seasoned founders will tell you that an entrepreneur's life can be all-consuming. So how do you prepare for it and keep it in perspective?

Envision living your life in a "wholistic" manner. View work as one component of your integrated life; think about how you will incorporate your entrepreneurial life into it.

Exercise 30: An Integrated Life

A Wholistic and Integrated Life		
Area	Ideal condition and goal	Action you're taking to achieve it
Personal • Mind • Body		
• Spirit • Heart • Finance		
Home (Family)		
Work		
Community		

CHAPTER RECAP

In this chapter, you spent much time in reflection and assessment.

- You've identified your sources of influence. You have an updated understanding of how they've inspired or inhibited you, how they've affected your attitudes and your decision-making process.

- You've assessed your habits and taken note of effective ones as well as recurrent challenges.

- You've reviewed accomplishments, best decisions, and winning approaches. You've analyzed failures. You've taken note of lessons learned.

- You've examined your window of beliefs, and understood how it influences your decision-making process.

- You've uncovered your internal and external sources of power. You know what you can access on your journey.

- You've affirmed your purpose and core values, and you've identified what/who grounds you and motivates you.

- You've evaluated your work-in-progress and have thought about how they may affect you in your founder role.

- You've recognized how a "wholistic" and integrated mindset can help you: 1) shift your present life into a strong and healthy position, 2) start your entrepreneurial life prepared, and 3) manage your entrepreneurial life so you don't lose perspective of the big picture.

Now that you've gone from introspection to assessment to articulation, you are more self-aware and self-engaged than before, and more integrated as you approach the next chapter: preparing for your founder role.

Chapter III:
Develop Founder Competency

Beginning is easy, continuing is hard.
Japanese Proverb

Starting a venture is easy. Operating it successfully is another story. As captain of your own vessel, you need to know seamanship before you embark on your entrepreneurial voyage. This means that you need to think about your own qualifications and start preparing for your founder role.

Most first-time founders who take the helm scarcely think about essential qualities that they—as skipper of their ship—should possess to ensure a smooth operation and success. Most are focused on developing their product idea. Many don't question their qualifications until they hit rough seas. Then they discover they lack qualities and/or skills needed to survive. Avoid this common and most serious oversight. Ensure that you'll begin with confidence and competence. So, what do you need to do to be ready?

Keep in Mind the Big Picture

Whether you're building a company of 10 or 1,000, you need to think about what kind of founder you will be. What functional roles will you perform throughout the venture's life cycle? Below are the main roles of a business entity. Titles vary depending on industry, but they're essentially the same. Keep this structure in mind as you research, assess, define, and develop your founder role.

Basic Organization - Top Level Structure

Founder
Is idea originator, visionary, cheerleader, product developer, launcher, builder, business developer, fund-raiser, and operator.

Chief Executive Office (CEO)
Is in charge of total management of a corporate entity. Main duties include: leader, manager, decision maker, communicator, cheerleader, and fund-raiser.

President
• Works closely with vice president, chief financial officer, and chief operating officer to implement the company's strategic plan.
• Modifies the company's strategy according to company needs, market trends, and economic conditions.
• Presides over the organization's day-to-day operations.

Chief Financial Officer (CFO)
Is responsible for financial planning and record keeping, and the company's financial health.

Chief Marketing Officer (CMO) / Vice President Marketing
Oversees research, product, communications, strategic planning, and customer service.

Chief of Technology (CTO) / Vice President Engineering
Is responsible for technological-related decisions and policy, which may include scientific research, company security, and customer privacy. In some cases, the CTO is also responsible for product strategy.

Vice President of Business Development
Oversees new business acquisitions, new market entries, and sales strategies.

Counsel
Ensures the business is compliant on various legal fronts: business filings, intellectual properties, labor law, environmental compliance, product compliance, and contract negotiations.

Recognize, Assess, and Plan Involvement During Your Venture

Your business will have four phases: preparation, start, growth, and exit. The following tasks may fall within these phases, depending on each business' unique needs, goals, and development pace. Review what needs to be accomplished and plan your involvement.

Four Phases

Preparation Phase
Founder development and preparation

Start Phase
- Ideation, research, and development
- Business formation, structure, standards, and processes
- Market research, customer profiling
- Concept refinement, prototype / product development, and launch

- Brand positioning, marketing, and business development
- Sales channel development
- Team building and talent management
- Operational expansion

Growth Phase
- Customer segmentation development
- New market research, prototypes, and product launches
- New sales channel development
- Team expansion
- Operational expansion

Exit Phase
Factors that may lead to your decision to exit
- You've achieved financial goals and want to sell
- You're bored and you want to sell
- Your market segment is saturated; consumption level remains flat
- Consumer demand is declining due to changing tastes
Preparation for sale / shut down

Think about how you will develop new skills and augment your founder's worth during various phases:

- Your founder role before your start,
- Your role(s) when you start,
- Your role(s) after you've started your venture (how you plan to develop it, strengthen it) and,
- Where you may be when you want to fold your business.

Now that you have the big picture in mind, focus on your first role and recognize that you need to serve as a role model who embodies standards that you want your crew to observe.

Develop Founder Competency

Earlier I pointed out that no training or certification is required to practice as an entrepreneur. Many first-time founders and co-founders put their best foot forward, but didn't know what they didn't know, unlike a physician or accountant. Because founders stumble, they need help preparing for their roles.

As your startup creator, you'll need what I call Founder IQ, which comprises essential tangible and intangible qualities and resources that enable you to take the helm as a competent skipper. Your Founder IQ is also an integral part of your founder's worth.

Most likely, you've already mastered some in a former or current job. Focus on those you need to strengthen. If you avoid those that make you uncomfortable, you'll weaken yourself. You may even lead your venture to crisis, if not failure. Review these skills and qualities; commit to developing competency before starting your venture.

Founder IQ
- Core action skills
- Core management skills
- Core qualities
- Financial preparedness
- Industry experience
- Survival skills

We begin with five core action skills required for your founder role.

The Founder's Core Action Skills
1. Initiate
2. Plan
3. Execute
4. Solve
5. Lead

Initiate

Personal initiative is the heart of starting and growing a new business, especially after the initial high at the launch. You'll need it to create opportunities, find customers and collaborators, and solve problems. You'll experience stops and starts, and that's when personal initiative is essential.

Founder Insights

Many founders are good at taking the initiative, but they are not so great at following through. Make sure you follow through.

The flip side of taking the initiative is knowing how to wait for an answer, wait for a development. Keeping options open may be the best strategy.

Plan

According to time management expert Alan Lakein, "We bring the future to the present by planning." Planning is actually more about strategic thinking than strategic planning. You can "plan" by making sure you possess the appropriate qualifications for your venture, and by gathering the tools and resources to help you solve whatever challenges may arise. You can create a road map, but given today's fast changing business conditions, make that Version 1.

Founder Insights

Sometimes, even though you thought you had prepared well, you realize that you are ill-equipped for a new situation. In this case, you "plan" by being ready to improvise, make do with what is available, and resolve that situation.

Execute

As founder, you need to implement your plans and accomplish your goals. You need to take action and move your venture forward.

Founder Insights

Impatient and overly confident founders rush ahead and execute without research or reflection. Insecure founders become paralyzed by fear and wait for someone else to make decisions. Knowing the right time to execute is important.

Solve

As founder, you are responsible for solving all issues that come your way, until you have a team to support you and you can delegate.

Founder Insights

Knowing your process for solving problems is essential. Recognizing how others solve problems helps you determine what is appropriate for your venture—from an immediate as well as long term perspective.

Lead

As a founder, you wear the leadership hat. You create the vision. You lead and inspire your team, keep them focused, and help them deliver. You must appear as a leader to all your collaborators—from investors to vendors—to ensure their support of your vision.

Some are born leaders. Even if you're a natural, there's room for growth. Others chafe at the thought of leading. If you recognize this in yourself, start developing your leadership skill now. Don't avoid it.

Founder Insights

A good leader is one who is accessible to your team, one whose presence provides stability and inspiration.

A true leader also knows when to lead and when to follow.

You don't discover what kind of leader you are until you're doing it. So give yourself some room for learning and growing.

Evaluate Your Founder's Core Action Skills

Clarify your attitude. When you think of each of the following skills, what emotion arises within you? Confidence? Discomfort? If it's the latter, it's a sign that you need to invest some time in it.

Think about how each skill informs your daily routine, decision-making process, and/or interaction with others. Where are you strongest? Where do you need to develop or improve? What action can you implement to strengthen your skills in your daily life as founder?

Exercise 31: Core Action Skills

Core Action Skills			
Skill	How often and how well do you employ this skill	Rate your skill (1 = weak; 2 = competent; 3 = strong; 4 = excellent)	Action to develop or refine
Initiate			
Plan			
Execute			

Core Action Skills			
Skill	How often and how well do you employ this skill	Rate your skill (1 = weak; 2 = competent; 3 = strong; 4 = excellent)	Action to develop or refine
Solve			
Lead			

Now you see where you're strongest in Core Action Skills and where you need to strengthen.

Next, take stock of where you stand with the following Core Management Skills.

The Founder's Core Management Skills

1. Self-management
2. Time management
3. Communication
4. Relationship management
5. Project management
6. Stress management
7. Crisis management
8. Financial management

All founders need these Core Management Skills. Now is a good time to review and assess. If you're already proficient, you've got a head start. If you feel tentative in certain areas, acknowledge them, then acquire confidence through practice. You don't need to excel at all of them before starting your venture (though it's great if you do), but you need to be proficient because they are essential to your success.

If there are areas where you feel you've already developed competency or expertise, skip them and move on to the next section.

Self-Management

As founder, you'll want to ensure you're able to manage personal and work fronts, before you can manage your crew and operation.

The Introspection exercises gave you a good sense of how your mind, body, heart, and spirit work together. They also illuminated the resources and habits you can tap for support, inspiration, and recharging, such as exercise, solitude, religious / spiritual practice, family, friends, and so on. They revealed areas you need to monitor or improve. In sum, they provided you with an integrated approach to self-management.

Time Management

As founder, you're creating not just a product, but a company with infrastructure, systems, and standards. You'll need good time management to make it happen in a timely way and keep it going.

Prior to founding your company, you might have been a professional in an established business. You might have found it easy to observe established working hours and deadlines. Now that you're at your own company, your work schedule will be yours. You're liberated from your structured corporate life. You may organize time as you see fit.

A first-time founder may experience a thrill of freedom, as work time is now under her control. After initial elation, she may find herself struggling to establish time management that works well. This is a common challenge for new founders.

As a new founder, you'll require more self-discipline than ever because you're the boss. You set and change schedules, deadlines, and performance metrics. Review how you spend your time, and plan to spend it wisely. You don't have time to waste; you want your business to run efficiently, and you must set an example. Research, assess, and customize your time management to your needs.

Founder Insights

View time as a friend instead of an adversary. Time is a resource, not something you have to conquer.

Recognize the difference between "urgent" and "important" and act accordingly. And note that a packed daily routine isn't necessarily an effective routine. You can be busy, but this doesn't mean that you're productive.

Respect your own time so you can set boundaries and make good use of it. If you don't set boundaries, others will and take away precious time from you.

Communication

As founder, you need to communicate well. A message not understood is a message not sent. Whether you're building a sole proprietorship or a Fortune 1000 company, communicating ideas effectively to your team, partners, and clients is key to success.

Founder Insights

We each communicate in our own unique way. It is important to know how you communicate as well as to recognize others' communication strengths and weaknesses.

Communication employs all your senses, and it's a two-way process. You can't communicate well if you don't listen well, if you're not attuned to your interlocutor's response. It is important to recognize how you deliver your message as well as how your audience responds to it. You need to be aware.

Relationship Management

Whether creating an individual proprietorship or a Fortune 1000 company, you need others to aid you. Ask for help when you need and be prepared to help when you can, when you're asked to help. Building and maintaining relationships is essential.

Founder Insights

Think of your relationships as a garden. If you want them to grow, you need to tend to them. You only have so many hours in a day, so cultivate the ones that inspire, enhance, and/or give you a chance to contribute, to make a difference. Focus on quality. Jettison the negative ones that deplete you.

Project Management

Excellent project management (PM) is a basic skill that should be taught in schools and required for anyone who embarks on a venture. Yet many founders don't take time to determine if they've good PM skills.

Many never establish PM standards. Some assume that individuals they hire for key positions—like head of sales, marketing, and client relations—are excellent project managers. Founders shouldn't assume this. You may have a great product idea, but without effective project managers, you and your team will encounter serious glitches.

As a founder, you will oversee activities that require competent project management. First, assess your own skill and acknowledge where you need to improve.

Establish standards and performance metrics. Every project needs a plan—whether a 5-step or 20-step plan—to ensure successful completion. Each plan needs a competent manager to execute—someone thoughtful, responsive, organized, and resourceful; who sees both the forest and the trees; who delivers.

Allocate energy, time, and resources for project management from Day One so that everyone you bring on board will have standards to observe. Without it, your venture will sail off course.

Founder Insights

Do not underestimate the importance of good project management. Your business needs all the parts working in concert. You need excellent project leaders to lead your team, establish meetings agendas, and manage the workflow that keeps your operation humming smoothly.

Stress Management

Starting a business is a thrilling and very stressful experience. Creating a new product, finding buyers, building a new team, and finding and allocating resources is not for the faint of heart. When you're a manager or a director, you're responsible for your department or section. When you're the founder, you're responsible for your entire crew and operation. Your stress level will increase. If you've already incorporated stress management habits into your daily life, that's great. If you've been struggling with this, now's the time to assess and prepare yourself.

Founder Insights

The harder you drive yourself and your team, the faster you'll achieve results. But if you don't take care of your own stress as founder and establish a stress management program for your team, you will burn out and so will they. Exhausted people do not make decisions clearly, nor do they perform to their potential.

Crisis Management

It's natural that an aspiring founder would be enthralled with his new business idea to the detriment of crisis management. But you will encounter crises, so you must think ahead, and develop or refine crisis management skills. Avoid being caught unprepared.

Founder Insights

Envision and prepare for various worst-case scenarios:

- What would you do if you had to fire a co-founder who happens to be one of your best friends? Or if you had to fire a family member, and this person has invested heavily in your venture, or holds a key position?

- What would you do if a competitor claimed that you stole his business idea or technology, and you had to halt operation, pending arbitration and a huge adjustment in your business strategy?

- What would you do if your key supplier shut down suddenly? Or the promotional materials for an upcoming launch, which you had ordered from an online printer, had incorrect dates and pricing info? What if you had budgeted for a purchase insufficiently?

- What would you do if your top salesperson suddenly quit in the middle of negotiations with an important client?

Do you have the confidence and poise to respond to whatever crises may occur? Or are you simply hoping you won't run into XYZ problems because you won't know how to resolve them?

Knowing how to remain calm and maintain poise during crises is key. Avoid making critical decisions during stressful moments. If you can, pause for a day, a week. Step away from the situation to obtain some perspective. Apply your personal powers: recognize you always have a choice. Even the least rewarding or the most difficult decision still entails a choice.

What skills, habits, and mental resources do you have at your disposal that will help you manage and solve crises?

Financial Management

In the Introspection section, you took stock of your personal financial habits. These will influence how you will deal with your company's finances. Now we take it one step further and help you prepare for your Finance role in your startup phase.

As founder, you are responsible for cash flow. You need to track expenses and revenues with an Excel spreadsheet or subscription to QuickBooks, an accounting software. If your professional experience includes finance and accounting, you've got a head start. If you don't, that's all right, too. Most first-time entrepreneurs aren't CPAs either.

At a minimum, acquire basic proficiency so you know how to manage your company's money. When you can afford it, hire a bookkeeper and an accountant to help you manage finances and prepare for tax payments. As business grows, you may delegate this responsibility to your CFO.

Take an accounting course online or at your local community college to develop basic competency. Read books on financial management for new businesses. Keep in mind there is no one definitive resource; every expert should cover the basics but also offer their unique insights.

Founder Insights

Always build in some financial cushion (especially if you're entering unfamiliar territory) for each project because most often, it will cost more than you originally anticipated. Double your estimates.

Assess Your Founder's Core Management Skills

Clarify your attitude. When you think of each of the following skills, what emotion arises within you? Confidence? Discomfort? If it's the latter, it's a sign that you need to invest some time in it.

Think about how each skill informs your daily routine, decision-making process, and/or interaction with others. Where are you strongest? Where do you need to develop or improve? What action can you implement to strengthen your skills in your daily life as founder?

Exercise 32: Core Management Skills

Core Management Skills			
Skill	How often and how well you employ this skill	Rate your skill (1 = weak; 2 = competent; 3 = strong; 4 = excellent)	Action to develop or refine
Self management			
Time management			
Communication			

Core Management Skills			
Skill	How often and how well you employ this skill	Rate your skill (1 = weak; 2 = competent; 3 = strong; 4 = excellent)	Action to develop or refine
Relationship management			
Project management			
Stress management			
Crisis management			
Financial management			

In additional to Core Management Skills, you'll need the following Core Qualities to help you prepare well for all kinds of situations that may arise. Assess your strengths and determine where you need to improve.

The Founder's Core Qualities

1. Self-awareness
2. Self-reliance
3. Discernment
4. Adaptability
5. Steadfastness
6. Perseverance
7. Optimism
8. Empathy

Self-awareness

Developing self-awareness isn't the first task that comes to mind for aspiring founders, but it's essential. I've worked with founders who lacked this quality. They didn't know how they behaved and appeared as business owner; they didn't recognize their worth, strengths, and weaknesses. They made critical decisions driven by ego or knee-jerk reaction, which contributed to startup failure.

Much of this book focuses on helping you develop it. It's the best gift you can give yourself. Self-awareness is a lifelong pursuit that each should undertake. Being self-aware means knowing:

- Where you came from: who and what influenced you in your personal and professional growth.
- Why you do what you do: what motivates you, what shuts you down. Who you are, and who you are not, and who you want to become as you evolve.
- What conditions enable you to be your best and what factors bring out your worst.
- What you need to take care of yourself well so you can take care of others.
- What you want to achieve: how you go about accomplishing it, what you are willing (or not willing) to do to realize it.

The more self-aware you are, the more attuned you'll be to your values, purpose, goals, strengths, and weak spots as you conduct business.

The more self-aware you are, the more aware you are of yourself in relation to others—how you appear, communicate, solve, and collaborate with others, and how they respond to you.

The more self-aware you are, the more you'll see which skills and resources you still need to acquire for your venture.

Founder Insights

Self-awareness alone does not lead to action, for one also needs self-confidence and personal initiative to act and affect change. Yet lack of self-awareness will surely to lead to blunders, if not failure.

Self-reliance

A self-reliant individual is one who: 1) knows her own powers and how to manage them, 2) has faith in her own judgment, and 3) possesses confidence in her ability to accomplish goals. A self-reliant mindset means possessing inner resources, trusting yourself to be someone you can depend on completely. It means counting on yourself to make things happen, solve problems, and create forward momentum.

Picture yourself as a captain on the high seas. Your satellite tracking system stops working, and no one on board can fix it. Do you sit there adrift, or do you reach for your sextant? Training yourself to be self-reliant will prepare you to solve problems and keep your venture on course.

If you were a part of an established corporate entity, you had a support system that helped you resolve a crisis. If one engineer got sick, another was available to substitute. If you needed research, your R&D department got it done. If you needed collateral, your marketing department produced them. If you needed a contract, your legal department cranked it out.

Most first-time founders will be bootstrapping during the first two years. You won't have a support system; you'll be the support system. You'll have to wear many hats while working with collaborators and suppliers.

Many inexperienced founders assume that help is a phone call or online search away. It's understandable, since today's technological offerings give us access to all kinds of immediate assistance. But many founders will experience crises when help isn't available because of lack of resources, money, or talent. While you may have advisors, friends, and family for advice, you'll experience many moments when you must take action alone.

Founder Insights

Self-reliance is not about not needing others' help; it's about ensuring you always have someone to rely on, especially during crises.

A self-reliant mindset sets the stage for your entrepreneurial journey so that you are emotionally, mentally, physically, and spiritually prepared to help yourself. It gives you a 24/7 a go-to person: you.

Discernment

A discerning individual possesses keen mental perception and understanding of people, situations, and environments. He can sift through hype and fluff to see what's beneath.

As founder, you'll need to navigate a sea of information overload, changing market conditions, and endless consumer demands. On a daily basis, you'll need to suss out the reality behind marketing and sales hype, recognize the difference between good and misplaced advice, and detect people's true motives behind false promises.

Adaptability

Founders need to be flexible and adapt to changes on their journey. Along with the willingness to adapt is the openness to change—and to ideas, solutions, and outcomes they might not have considered.

Some co-founders were so sold on their products they were unwilling to adapt to a new generation of consumers. One startup went from occupying the leader position in their market to falling behind because they refused to adapt to changing tastes.

Founders need to adapt or they may miss timely opportunities and take a tumble. Worse, if they're not open to change and fail to adapt, they may not survive.

Founder Insights

A part of being adaptable is knowing when it's prudent to adjust pace and path. It's knowing when you need to move and when you need to wait.

Like the sea captain who needs to adjust to changing weather, you may find that you'll need to adapt to sudden changes in suppliers, market conditions, customer tastes, and technology.

Steadfastness

As founder, you may face changing customer tastes that force you to reassess your course. You may encounter crises that threaten to bring down your business. You'll need faith, a steady mind, and stout heart to stay firm in your purpose and conviction, and to focus on problem solving.

As you build your business, you'll need help from family, friends, former colleagues, collaborators, and suppliers. As you depend on them to be responsive and reliable to help you succeed, you'll need to return the favor and demonstrate the same kind of dependability.

Founder Insights

Be unwavering in your purpose, steadfast in your pursuit of your vision. Avoid external distractions.

Demonstrate your firm commitment and unwavering support to anyone from whom you expect such reciprocity.

Perseverance

The entrepreneurial voyage is always longer than what most first-time founders anticipate. It requires perseverance.

You'll experience operational glitches, supply delays, hardware malfunctions, employee grievances, and hacking.

Potential business partners and investors may reject you. You may come across non-believers who question everything about you, your product, and your venture.

You must hold your course, persevere through rough patches, solve your problems, and move forward.

Founder Insights

In the startup landscape, problems need to be resolved quickly. Speed is expected and so is perseverance. Yet speed takes center stage while perseverance plods along silently behind, until results are delivered. In the end, what matters the most is faith in your entrepreneurial journey and willingness to endure—including through challenging times. These are what it takes to realize your dream.

Optimism

An optimist views a situation, condition, or event favorably. She leans toward the view that all will end on a positive note.

It is easy to be enthusiastic and positive when you're starting out. When you encounter obstacles and lose momentum, that's when you need faith. You'll need an optimist's resolve to find a silver lining and solutions. You'll need an optimist's confidence to create momentum and kick-start a stalled process. Pessimists have a harder time moving past challenges.

Martin Seligman, a psychologist at the University of Pennsylvania, has researched happiness and found that optimism and pessimism are learned behaviors. If you're a pessimist, think about how your responses to past challenges turned out. Were results satisfactory?

If you note a pattern of unsatisfactory results based on your outlook, step away from your comfort zone and think how an optimist would respond or act. But don't be a Pollyanna; wearing rose-colored glasses doesn't work either.

Founder Insights

As founder, you must cultivate optimism and be your own cheerleader. Your venture is your dream, your vision. If you lack an optimist's outlook, you won't be able to rally and convince others in your company to stay and support you during difficult times.

Last, but not least...

Empathy

As founder, you'll interact with all kinds of individuals; they include those you hire to be your crew, your strategic partners, suppliers, consultants, and investors. Your ability to identify with other people's thoughts, feelings, and viewpoints—putting yourself in their shoes—will help you to communicate and manage various relationships better.

Evaluate Your Founder's Core Qualities

Clarify your attitude. When you think of each of the following qualities, what emotion arises within you? Confidence? Discomfort? If it's the latter, it's a sign that you need to invest some time in it.

Think about how each quality informs your daily routine, decision-making process, and/or interaction with others. Where are you strongest? Where do you need to develop or improve? What action can you implement to strengthen your skills in your daily life as founder?

Exercise 33: Core Qualities

Core Qualities			
Quality	How often and how well do you tap into this quality	Rate your level (1 = weak; 2 = competent; 3 = strong; 4 = excellent)	Action to develop or refine
Self-awareness			
Self-reliance			
Discernment			
Adaptability			
Steadfastness			
Perseverance			

Core Qualities			
Quality	How often and how well do you tap into this quality	Rate your level (1 = weak; 2 = competent; 3 = strong; 4 = excellent)	Action to develop or refine
Optimism			
Empathy			

If you need to strengthen one or two critical founder skills, you can manage this while starting your company. If, after reflection, research, and assessment, you conclude you still have five or more skills to develop, you should consider taking classes, self-teaching, or a job where you can acquire these while getting paid. You may be courageous for wanting to "wing it" by starting your venture without many critical skills, but you should avoid taking the helm without having developed competency in most of them. It's wise to spend time training and being prepared.

Startup Anecdotes

Before starting my first business, I worked for five established companies: an investment bank, a management consulting firm, two wireless service providers, and a family business. I learned about infrastructure, standards of operations, processes, and different corporate cultures and management styles. I picked up best practices and pitfalls to avoid. These helped me set up my first operation without startup chaos.

That said, starting a new business is one thing, but running it is another. I discovered that even though I was in charge, I lacked certain functional skills.

I had built a new company and knew I had to promote it, but I tensed each time I thought of business development. I understood why I chafed at selling; I had grown up in a culture that prizes academic achievement and relegates selling to the bottom of the ladder. The stereotype about sleazy sales people was ingrained in my psyche.

I spent time reading, talking to mentors, and trying to improve my sales skills. I struggled to wear the Sales hat without feeling I was faking it. I learned to leverage my natural instinct to be helpful and I looked for opportunities where I could contribute. It took me a long time to stop cringing at contacting potential clients. Today I would say I've developed competency, but I'd never hire myself as head of a business development team. It's not my forte, but neither is it my Achilles heel.

So, if you know what your weak spot is, commit time and energy to address it.

The Founder's Financial Preparedness

You've examined your financial habits. Now review your financial situation, and think about how your venture will affect your financial standing.

Exercise 34: Financial Preparedness

1. How much money have you saved?
2. How much money will you set aside and not touch, under ANY circumstances?
3. How much money do you need to cover monthly basic needs while you work on your venture?
4. How much money will you invest to start your venture?
5. Will you invest to keep it going until break-even or profitable stage?

6. At what point will you stop financing your business if your product doesn't attract buyers?
7. How much money will you allocate for emergency needs for the venture?
8. At what point will you need to raise money? How much do you plan to raise? How much of your company would you give up?
9. How will you use the proceeds?
10. Ultimately, how much control of the company do you plan to maintain?
11. When do you expect to see a return on your investment? In five years? Ten years?

If you plan to finance your business, you're in complete financial control of your operation.

If you plan to seek additional money, familiarize yourself with the financial landscape before your start your venture. Understand what you're giving away, when you raise money. Be informed before you offer equity to a co-founder or a new team member.

Today's founders have multitude of financial resources. Yet, very few research all options prior to embarking on their venture. Many first-timers set aside a startup budget to get the company going or prove their product idea. In their mind, they will research and figure out where the rest of the money comes from once they've started. Many founders shut down operations because cash flow hasn't turned positive.

To avoid this outcome, you need to research and study all the financing options available to new business owners. Read books on how to finance a new business. Find titles at your local library, your local bookstore, or online stores. Visit the SBA website for financing resources. Some local SBA offices also offer classes for entrepreneurs. Talk to local bankers, lenders, angel investors, and venture capitalists. Research their websites.

Learn about financing options before you embark—so that you have all of this information at your disposal and can incorporate that into your short-term as well as long-term plans.

Plan ahead. Let's say that in Year 3 or Year 4, you decide that the entrepreneurial life is not for you. Will you have set aside money to do something else? Will you have some financial cushion while you're taking a break or looking for a new career direction?

Don't start your business without this preparation.

The Founder's Industry Experience

Every job you've ever performed has contributed to where you are to-day. There's value in learning what you're good at and discovering what doesn't suit you. Take out your most recent resume. Review it, and update it. Extract for the following exercise.

- What experience and insights did you obtain from the industries that you've worked in?
- Which industry knowledge and experience can you apply to your founder role?
- What new experience and skills will you need to develop for your venture?

Exercise 35: Industry Experience

Industry Experience		
Industry	Functional experience / skill	Achievement / Failure / Insight
1.		
2.		
3.		

You will have more resources and insights at your disposal, if you possess deep knowledge of the industry in which you're planning to sell your product.

It may be worthwhile to acquire industry experience by working for someone else first. Otherwise, you'll have to spend time, energy, money, and resources learning an entirely new market niche.

The Founder's Survival Skills

You're excited about your new business idea and raring to start developing it. Survival skills aren't on your to-do list. But proper planning prevents poor performance. Know what survival tools you need in addition to your founder skills and qualities.

Most inexperienced founders rarely give much thought to what may go wrong. Many have this simplistic view of the road to success: build the prototype, find paying customers, build a client base, find investors, and expand. But unexpected problems loom large, and small problems crop up all along the way.

You can't prepare for all scenarios, but as a qualified founder, your self-reliant mindset and survival skills will help you face challenges. You need to envision the best outcome, the realistic outcome, and the worst outcome. Conduct scenario planning. What can go wrong while you're on the high seas? What do you need to do if you lack tools to fix a leak or run out of supplies, or have to deal with a troublesome crew member? How will you resolve worst-case scenarios?

You've spent time in the Introspection section reacquainting yourself with your sources of influence, beliefs, values, habits, and purpose. You've identified powers and strengths. You've recalled successes and failures. You need resources that you can access anytime, anywhere: those resources reside within you. As you progress through this book and accompanying exercises, think about what to add to your Survival Kit.

Example: Founder Brooke's Survival Kit
• Excellence with logistics • Tactile skills • Negotiation skills • Patience • Optimism • Self-reliance • Calm and poise during crisis • Unconventional ways of doing things

Exercise 36: Founder's Survival Kit

Over the next few weeks, think about what you will add to your Survival Kit. What are your must-haves?

CHAPTER RECAP

In this chapter, you've focused on founder competency, in particular, your own Founder IQ. You've assessed your core skills and qualities, financial preparedness, industry knowledge, and survival skills. You know what you need to strengthen or develop. You've recognized the need to think about and plan for the four phases of your venture.

You've also had an opportunity to think further about how you'll fortify your founder's worth. First-time founders seldom realize that their worth is something that they need to articulate, affirm and build throughout their entrepreneurial journey. For many, because they are unaware of it, they inadvertently give potential investors an edge. Define your worth before someone else does it for you.

Chapter IV:
Review, Assess, and Choose
Your Next Move

The Navigator has brought to your attention the importance of your founder role. It has shown you the need to prepare well as founder, before embarking on an entrepreneurial journey.

You've learned that, while your product idea and business model may evolve, the constant you want and need on your journey is you. As founder and product creator, you hold great responsibility and wield immense power. Founder competency—including self-reliance—is essential because you are responsible for your product and operation. You are the one who is always accessible to you for support, troubleshooting, resolving, and moving your venture along.

The Navigator has introduced you to an integrated mindset and approach that help you develop, lead, and grow as a founder during your journey.

It's all about execution. That's why the more qualified and prepared you are, the higher the chance you will succeed.

The following exercises should help you identify where you are and decide your next move.

The Integrated You

At the start of your founder development, you took a Snapshot of Where You Are Today in Chapter III; review the answers you provided. Now that you've completed Introspection and various exercises, let's see where you are today.

Exercise 37: A Snapshot of Where You Are Today, Post-Introspection and Integration

1. What new awareness have you acquired about yourself (sources of influence, habits, beliefs, and untapped skills), about your new business idea, and/or about your venture? List 3-5 useful insights have you acquired.

2. How have your insights, priorities, and goals for this year and next year changed? What are your revisions?

3. Knowing what you do now about how to develop your founder role and how to prepare for your startup, do you still feel pulled toward your new business idea? Is it still compelling? Is this a must-do?

4. Envision what your daily routine will look like, how your startup life will fit into the rest of your personal life.

5. The entrepreneurial voyage is a life-changing experience. Are you ready to transform your life?

6. What conditions need to be in place in order for you to feel ready to start this venture?

Founder Readiness		
Area	Condition that needs to be in place	Assess your readiness: (1 = not ready; 2 = almost ready, but need to accomplish a few tasks / learn new skills; 3 = ready to start)
Mind		
Body		
Spirit		
Heart		
Finance		

The Founder Section

Review your Founder IQ:
- **Core action skills**: initiate, plan, execute, solve, and lead.
- **Core management skills**: self-management, time management, communication, relationship management, project management, stress management, crisis management, and financial management.
- **Core qualities**: self-awareness, self-reliance, discernment, adaptability, steadfastness, perseverance, optimism, and empathy.
- **Financial preparedness**
- **Industry experience**
- **Survival skills**

Exercise 38: Assess Your Readiness in the Founder Role

1. What core qualities, skills, sources of power, habits, and insights are helping you feel most confident, most ready to proceed as founder?

Factor (quality / skill / habit)	Examples that show you are in top form
1.	
2.	
3.	

2. What recurrent challenges and new issues (those that emerged during your Introspection exercises) do you need to keep in mind as you start the venture?

Factor (quality / skill / habit)	What you need to monitor
1.	
2.	
3.	

3. What core qualities, skills, and habits do you still need to develop or refine BEFORE starting your venture?

Factor (quality / skill / habit)	What you need to develop
1.	
2.	
3.	

4. Identify three goals that you want to accomplish in order to build your worth as founder.

5. Review your financial preparedness.

6. Identify three factors that might derail you during the first two years if you are not careful.

7. Envision your worst-case scenario: business failure. How will you move forward? What cushions will you have in place for yourself?

8. Review your Survival Kit. What physical tools, what intangible tools are your must-haves?

9. How qualified do you feel today, after introspection and integration?
   • Not qualified; need to research and reflect some more.
   • Somewhat qualified and need to develop some essential skills.
   • Qualified and ready to start.

10. Create your short To-Do List. Set clear goals for your first and second years. Assign yourself weekly and monthly tasks. Focus and execute.

11. Monitor your progress frequently. Make time to review your achievements, as well as your personal and founder's goals.
    • Rate your performance and take note of areas to be refined or strengthened.
    • Take note of lessons learned and insights gained.
    • Update your goals and start anew.

Keep in mind that no singular startup model works for all; each venture is a trial-and-error voyage of adjustment and refinement. There's no "right age" to become an entrepreneur. The right time for you is when you feel ready. Hopefully, this is when you feel that: 1) all parts of your life—mind, body, heart, and spirit—are in good if not excellent shape, and 2) you are well positioned with resources to integrate your startup's life into your daily life.

The Navigator has focused on helping you develop essential founder skills before you embark on your entrepreneurial journey. Another important issue that you'll need to address is how to establish the infrastructure to support both your product development and startup operation. I've addressed this issue in my book, *The Founder's Manifest - For Anyone Starting a Business*. Remember that working for a startup is different than running a startup. If you lack this knowledge, I encourage you to read *TFM*. In the meantime, I've included below a Master Checklist to help you get started.

Your Master Checklist

Create the following checklist to keep focused. Extract it for your business plan and investment deck—when you prepare for potential investors.

Exercise 39: Master Checklist

Master Checklist
Business Name and Description

Product
- What problem and/or need does it address?
- How much does it cost to create it?
- How long does it take to create it?
- How eco-friendly is it?
- Who uses it?
- Who pays for it?
- How much will you charge to break even? To make a profit?
- What is your expected profit margin?
- How will you sell it?
- Where will you sell it?

Crew
- How well prepared are you as ship captain?
- Where do you need help?
- How will you obtain help?
- How long will it take to get help?
- How much are you paying for help?

- What kind of people will be right for your crew?
- What compensation structure will you have in place for your team?

Infrastructure
- What is your company culture?
- What is its organizational structure?
- What standards, systems, and processes do you have in place?

Finance
- How will you finance your prototype and later, startup operation?
- How much startup money will you have?
- How long before you run out of startup money, before your first sale?
- Have you researched all your financing options?
- Are you prepared to manage your accounts until you hire full-time help?

Your Critical Role
- How will you build your worth as founder through each phase?
- How will you manage yourself: stay in shape, keep yourself focused, and run a tight ship?
- How will you manage daily stress, unanticipated crises?
- How will you manage and lead your team?

Scenario Planning
- What are your venture's best-case, realistic-case, and worst-case scenarios?
- What's in your Survival Kit?
- How do you define venture success?
- What constitutes failure?
- What does your life look like beyond your startup up life?

Conclusion

You've spent time reading, reflecting, researching, and doing exercises. This has given you the opportunity to know yourself on mental, emotional, spiritual, physical, and financial levels. You have the knowledge and insights to develop and grow as a founder.

Now you can decide how you want to move forward. Moving forward can mean that you want to pursue your entrepreneurial path. While you will learn much on the job, it is prudent to start as well prepared as you can. Remember that it takes time, energy and commitment to develop your founder role. Train with *The Navigator* and use it as your guide. Your great business idea depends on how well you execute as founder.

Alternatively, moving forward can mean that you're not ready to strike out on your own, or that the entrepreneurial path is not for you. Both are legitimate decisions, if informed.

I wish you the best, whether that means seeing your current career path in a new light or embarking on a new journey.

My-Tien Vo
San Francisco
California
2018

Notes

1. The New Shorter Oxford English Dictionary, Oxford University Press 1993.

2. Worth: usefulness or importance, as to the world, to a person, or for a purpose. Source: dictionary.com. (Accessed August 25, 2012).

3. Alan Lakein, *How to Get Control of Your Time and Your Life* (Penguin Books USA Inc., 1973), 49.

4. Pareto Principle. Source: en.wikipedia.org/wiki/Pareto_principle. (Accessed August 25, 2012).

5. Power: ability to do or act; capability of doing or accomplishing something. Source: Dictionary.com. (Accessed August 25, 2012).

Founder Resources

Below are book series, titles, and links that you might find useful.

Brilliant Series publish business books that cover a variety of subjects, from project management to marketing to branding to selling. (pearsoned.co.uk/bookshop/subject.asp?item=9655).

Nolo Series (nolo.com) publish informative business and legal books, which cover numerous topics, including *Legal Forms for Starting & Running a Business, Tax Savvy for Small Business, Contracts, and Working for Yourself.*

Small Business Administration (sba.gov) offers information on business structures, business licenses, loans and grants, business financials, and tax filings.

TED Talks (ted.com) - Information and inspiration.

Business
- Jim Collins and Jerry I. Porras, *Built to Last: Successful Habits of Visionary Companies*
- Jim Collins, *Good to Great: Why Some Companies Make the Leap and Others Don't*
- Guy Kawasaki and Lindsey Filby, *The Art of the Start 2.0*

Communication and Presentation
- Amy Jen Su and Murial Maignan Wilkins, *Own the Room*
- Duarte offers an array of presentation templates (duarte.com/ free-presentation-software-templates/)
- Deborah Gruenfeld on Power and Influence (womensleadership. stanford.edu/power)

Creativity
- Michael J. Gelb, *How to Think like Leonardo da Vinci*
- Brewster Ghiselin, *The Creative Process*
- Robert Grudin, *The Grace of Great Things*
- Rollo May, *The Courage to Create*

Crisis Management
- Harvard Business Essential, *Crisis Management: Mastering the Skills to Prevent Disasters*
- Steven Fink, *Crisis Communications: Planning for the Inevitable*
- Steve Tobak, *How to Manage a Crisis, Any Crisis* (cnet.com/news/ how-to-manage-a-crisis-any-crisis/)

Finance
- Scott L. Girard, Jr., Michael F. O'Keefe, Marc A. Price, *Business Finance Basics*
- Mark Suster - Both Sides of the Table (bothsidesofthetable.com)
- Funders and Founders (fundersandfounders.com)
- Go4Funding (go4funding.com)
- How Startup Funding Works (fundersandfounders.com/ how-funding-works-splitting-equity)

Leadership
- Terry R. Bacon, *Elements of Influence*
- Stephen Denning, *The Leader's Guide to Storytelling*
- Deborah Gruenfeld on Power and Influence (womensleadership. stanford.edu/power)
- Stephen E. Kohn and Vincent D. O'Connell, *6 Habits of Highly Effective Bosses*

- Derek Lidow, *How Savvy Entrepreneurs Turn Their Ideas Into Successful Enterprises*
- Nan S. Russell, *The Titleless Leader*

Nonprofit
- Smith, Buckling & Associates, Inc. *The Complete Guide to Nonprofit Management*

Personal Development
- Marcus Aurelius, *Meditations* (Translated by Maxwell Staniforth)
- Joseph Campbell, *The Power of Myth*
- Joseph Campbell, *The Hero with a Thousand Faces*
- Chang Po-Tuan, *The Inner Teachings of Taoism* (Translated by Thomas Cleary)
- Stephen R. Covey, *The 7 Habits of Highly Effective People*
- Angela Duckworth, *Grit*
- Charles Duhigg, *Why We Do What We Do in Life and Business*
- Carol S. Dweck, Ph.D., *Mindset - The New Psychology of Success*
- Daniel Goleman, *Emotional Intelligence*
- Robert Grudin, *The Grace of Great Things*
- Allen F. Harrison and Robert M. Bramson, Ph.D., *Styles of Thinking*
- Carl C. Jung, *Man and His Symbols*
- Caroline Myss, *Archetypes*
- Carol Pearson, *Awakening the Heroes Within*
- Richard Strozzi-Heckler, *Holding The Center*
- MBTI 16 Personalities (16personalities.com)
- Thich Nhat Hanh, *Peace Is Every Step - The Path of Mindfulness in Everyday life*
- Lane Wallace, *Surviving Uncertainty*

Power
- Terry R. Bacon, *The Elements of Power: Lessons on Leadership and Influence*
- Deborah Gruenfeld on Power and Influence (womensleadership.stanford.edu/power)

- Nicholas H. Morgan, *Power Cues*
- Jeffrey Pfeffer, *Power - Why Some People Have It And Others Don't*

Project Management
- Scott Berkun, *The Art of Project Management*
- Kory Kogon, Suzette Blakemore, James Wood, *Project Management for the Unofficial Project Manager*

Sales
- Marion Luma Bream, *Women Make the Best Salesmen*
- Kim MacPherson, *Permission-based E-Mail Marketing That Works!*
- Tom Martin, *The Invisible Sale*
- Ron Willingham, *Authenticity – The Head, Heart, and Soul of Selling*

Social Entrepreneurship
- Robert J. Rosenthal and Greg Baldwin, *Volunteer Engagement 2.0*

Startups
- Best Pitches (bestpitchdecks.com)
- Bloomberg U.S. Startups Barometer (bloomberg.com/graphics/startup-barometer)
- Scott Duffy, *Launch!: The Critical 90 Days from Idea to Market*
- Funders and Founders (fundersandfounders.com)
- Richard Stim and Lisa Guerin, *Wow! I am in Business*
- Mark Suster - Both Sides of the Table (bothsidesofthetable.com)
- NY Times Entrepreneurship (nytimes.com/pages/business/small-business)
- OnStartups (onstartups.com)
- Noam Wasserman, *The Founder's Dilemmas*

Talent Management
- Lou Adler, *Hire With Your Head*
- Dr. Joy Bodzioch, *Catching the Wave of Workforce Diversity*
- Amy DelPo and Lisa Guerin, *Create Your Own Employee Handbook*
- Mary B. Holihan, *Human Resources for the Small Business Owner*

- Mark Murphy, *Hiring for Attitude*
- Geoff Smart and Randy Street, *Who - The A Method for Hiring*
- Brad Feld and Mahendra Ramshinghani, *Startup Boards*

Thinking and Decision-Making Process
- Rolf Dobelli, *The Art of Thinking Clearly*
- Charles Duhigg, *The Power of Habit*
- John S. Hammond, *Smart Choices*
- Joseph T. Hallinan, *Why We Make Mistakes*
- Daniel Kahneman, *Thinking, Fast and Slow*
- Allen F. Harrison and Robert M. Bramson, Ph.D., *The Art of Thinking*
- Jonah Lehrer, *How We Decide*
- Rod Judkins, *The Art of Creative Thinking*

Time Management / Productivity
- David Allen, *Getting Things Done* (gettingthingsdone.com)
- Robert Grudin, *Time and The Art of Living*
- Alan Lakein, *How to Get Control of Your Time and Your Life*
- Carson Tate (carsontate.com)

•••

About the Author

My-Tien Vo is a founder coach, startup consultant, and brand strategist who has worked closely with founders, co-founders, and startup teams from various industries. They include construction, education, electrical, healthcare, hospitality, legal, nonprofit, professional services, real estate, retail, and technology. She has been immersed in the startup landscape since 1998—as founder, co-founder, product manager, brand strategist, content developer, founder coach, team builder, e-commerce director, researcher, and crisis manager.

Her work with founders has led to many successful launches and also a share of stalled operations. As an integral member of many startup teams, Vo has had first-hand experience of what works and what doesn't work. She felt compelled to share her entrepreneurial insights after one of her startups failed—in spite of possessing many winning attributes. What began as an essay for her blog has evolved into *The Founder's Manifest - For Anyone Starting a New Business*, a founder-centric guide for launching a new company.

Her second book, *The Navigator*, presents an integrated mindset and approach to help aspiring entrepreneurs develop Founder Competency—skills and qualities needed to increase their chances of success with both product launch and startup operation.

Prior to embarking on her entrepreneurial path, Vo worked for an investment bank, an international management consulting firm, wireless service providers, and a family-owned business. Her corporate experiences proved a valuable asset to her startup endeavors. Vo earned a B.A. with Honors from Brown University and a M.A.L.D from The Fletcher School of Law and Diplomacy.